D1108380

The Sound & The Fury

Warner Troyer

The Sound & The Fury

AN ANECDOTAL HISTORY OF
CANADIAN BROADCASTING

 John Wiley & Sons Canada Limited

Copyright © 1980, Warner Troyer

ALL RIGHTS RESERVED. No part of this publication may be repro-
duced, stored in a retrieval system or transmitted in any form or
by any means electronic, mechanical, photocopying, recording or
otherwise, without the prior written permission of the publishers.

*The publisher has made every effort to give accurate credit to
the sources of illustrations which appear in this book. In the event
of error or omission, notification would be appreciated.*

Personal Library, Publishers
Suite 439
17 Queen Street East
Toronto, Canada   M5C 1P9

Publisher: Glenn Edward Witmer
Editor: Sarah Swartz Consultant Services
Research: Glenys Moss
Production Editor: Catherine Van Baren
Composition: Canadian Composition Limited
A PEPPERMINT DESIGN

A Personal Library publication
produced exclusively for
John Wiley and Sons Canada Limited
22 Worcester Road, Rexdale, Ontario
M9W 1L1

Canadian Cataloguing in Publication Data

Troyer, Warner, 1932-
  The sound and the fury

Includes index.
ISBN 0-471-99872-9

1. Radio broadcasting — Canada — History.
2. Television broadcasting — Canada — History.
I. Title.

HE8689.9.C2T76   384.54   C80-094060-1

Printed and bound in Canada

Contents

This book is for
PETER REILLY *and* NORMAN DEPOE
the best of a good lot.

Peter Reilly
(CBC Archives)

Norman DePoe
(CBC Archives)

Preface

One of my children remarked, after the publication of my last book, "You can say anything you like in a preface, Dad, 'cause nobody ever reads that dull junk at the beginning; they just want to read the book." Someone else has suggested that prefaces are generally used by authors to excuse the shortcomings that follow in the ingenuous hope of thereby disarming book reviewers and other critics.

What follows here is self-evident; no reader will need my excuses or my help in locating any merits or failures. But for those who *do* read introductions, a very brief word:

First, this book is not, nor is it intended to be, any sort of definitive or encyclopaedic history; it is peripatetic, anecdotal and, above all, subjective. The bibliography will direct students of Canadian broadcasting to many of the voluminous studies which describe the political, philosophical and economic progressions of our broadcast system. Authoritatively done, just a history of the political machinations of Canadian radio and TV would require at least one massive tome per decade. The purpose here has been to make some of the colour, pageantry and irony of our broadcast experience accessible and entertaining.

About the "subjectivity": objective reporting is, to me, as improbable as a self-lubricating, perpetual motion machine. The only apparently genuine objective journalism I've ever encountered involved the use of a computer which pronounced a weather forecast in portentous but rather hard to understand tones. Even then there'd been subjective input earlier — from the meteorologist who decided which isobars he took seriously; and the programmer who selected the portions of the forecast to be fed into the computer and thereby censored those omitted.

I've long believed there's a "fourth dimension" to reporting: that a journalist who takes seriously the trade of being surrogate to his/her readers/listeners/viewers should, after reporting *what* is happening and *why*, go on, when the forum is appropriate, to add a personal response. If the prime minister was intoxicated while making the speech, that's information which the reporter was privileged to acquire by reason of being physically present. If the tearful reunion of two former political adversaries on a public platform was accompanied by a glacial air of antipathy between their aides, that *feeling* is part of the story. Moreover, it's part of the rich experience we journalists are permitted only because we are surrogates for our readers and listeners. We owe them the evidences of our senses and our glands as well as the hard facts.

Beyond all of that, my own activities in broadcasting, reaching back to the late forties, have involved me too deeply and too intimately with this peculiar industry to permit my being detached. I could not, even if I wished, ape the theologians of earlier times who wished to be "in this world, but not of it." Broadcast journalism has shaped me as surely as I've shaped some small corners of it, if only by the way we've constantly rubbed against one another. So for the personal anecdotes, recollections, judgements, no apology but merely an acknowledgement of their presence and a declaration of my conviction that they have a place.

Thirty-plus years after my first ludicrous experiments with a wire recorder (tape came later), I'm still persuaded that God never intended for sounds and pictures to fly through the air, given the obstacles She puts in their way. But it's a helluva lotta fun trying.

It remains, just to be certain that *someone* reads the introduction, to thank C. Alexander Brown for his measureless aid in both editorial and pictorial research, Glenys Moss who provided those same services together with her utterly indispensable personal support, encouragement and unerring editorial judgement, and the host of broadcasters, professional and occasional, who shared their experience, the priceless photos from their private collections, and their wisdom; and my very special thanks to the unsung heroes of Canada's National Archives and to the guardians of CBC's print and photo libraries. This is, for what it's worth, their book.

Surviving Geography

Every nation state has its albatross, usually one forged by history. Canada's, ever present, is obvious, proximate, and ubiquitous. Mackenzie King put it most simply, in a debate in the House of Commons on June 18, 1936, "If some countries have too much history, we have too much geography."

That was scarcely news. O. D. Skelton, the creator and founder of our Department of External Affairs in later years, noted in 1916, "That the present Canada is not a natural geographic unit is an undeniable fact." In 1911 William Lawson Grant, historian and soon to become headmaster of Upper Canada College, remarked that "in Canada, man is making a nation in defiance of geographical conditions." As Laurier himself had said in 1887, "You cannot legislate against geography." Even Rabelais, searching for a hyperbolic metaphor for size, in 1548 had written of an object, "not less large than Canada."

The point bears labouring, even belabouring. Canada *should* be pre-eminent throughout the world in the fields most vital to our common and community survival: transportation and communication. Without either, we endure as a disparate, balkanized group of parochial regions, united chiefly in our familial mistrust, our mutual fear of influences beyond our control, and our common anxiety to avoid being served the smallest portions at our political, corporate boarding-house table.

We've tried, of course. Despite the kidney-crushing roadbeds used by Via Rail and Air Canada's best efforts to approximate conditions on an east European bus service, we do have a national transportation system. Nor have the worst efforts of network producers bent on self-aggrandizement, or network bureaucrats obsessed with "audience enjoyment indices," managed to prevent our establishment of the physical hardware needed to carry radio and television programming into most of the corners, cloisters and crannies of our national community. That may be the chief irony: we've the hardware but never have had the will and the wit to make our radio and television services work effectually against the continuing isolation and fragmentation of our Canadian psyche.

Both technically and creatively, Canadians have outrun those in other nations more often than we could expect or should deserve on grounds either of population and wealth or of purpose and support. But we've generally appeared chiefly as a procession of the bland leading the bland through our mindless acceptance of a catechism of misconceptions:

a) We've come, mistakenly, to equate unity with centralism.
b) We've been persuaded, by the two-dimensional Canadian clones of Madison Avenue, Hollywood and the like to confuse spectacle with merit.
c) We've assumed that no region of Canada is likely to be deeply interested in the alien experiences and culture of another; all of this while witnessing the stunning audience interest across Canada in "Roots," "I, Claudius," "Upstairs, Downstairs," and "Star Trek." (We tried with "Jalna" and bombed. In 1979 "A Gift to Last" worked better.)
d) We've encouraged regional programming to die of attrition and disinterest, or worse, left it to add to the sum of encapsulated broadcast solitudes dividing our culture.

Kate Reid, probably Canada's finest dramatic actress, mounted in a drama even her skill couldn't save from inept production and editing: "Jalna." (CBC Archives)

Gordon Pinsent, writer and star of "A Gift To Last" with his fictional TV nephew, Mark Polley. (CBC Archives)

e) We've carefully blunted our own nerve ends and
   denied our own heritage so as to be better able
   to slavishly imitate U.S. and British programming;
   this on the wholly improbable ground that
   Canadian listeners and viewers would prefer
   watered-down, low-budget imitations to the real
   thing, to which they already have easy and
   immediate access.

The result of all of this, as evidenced by perusal
of radio and TV rating surveys in Canada, is
that the most common response to broadcasting,
wherever one goes in Canada, is the sound of one
hand clapping.

RADIO

Many Canadian listeners made their own crystal sets, but for the affluent, Canadian General Electric sold this set in its

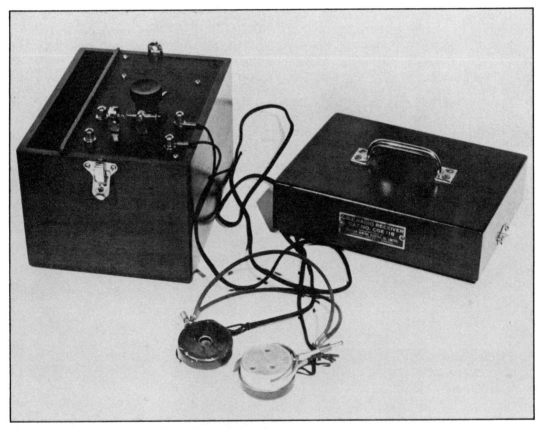

handsome wooden case in 1922-23. (National Museum of Science and Technology, Ottawa)

"Testing: One, two, three, four…" 1900-1929

The first broadcast by radio waves of a human voice was made by a Canadian. What moves that experience back into the realm of the ordinary and predictable is the knowledge that:

a) The experiment took place in the United States with American funding.

b) The inventor, forever frustrated in his efforts to get Canadian support, died in Bermuda a bitter and mostly unrecognized man.

c) The Canadian government, while denying assistance to the most brilliant man in the field, a Canadian, was busily funding and supporting an Italian inventor.

d) Finally, in an awesome blend of genius and banality, our intrepid inventor, making the first broadcast of a human voice in all of recorded history, uttered the stunning words, "one, two, three, four." Every public announce system tester in the time since owes him a debt of gratitude.

My own earliest memory of broadcasting comes from the thirties, when many Canadians had a crystal set, probably in their kitchen. The first set I saw, in someone else's home, was quickly covered by a newspaper or tea towel when there was a knock at the back door. It might have been an inspector from the Federal Department of Marines and Fisheries who, finding any home radio receivers, would demand payment of the one-dollar annual licence fee used by the government to regulate broadcasting, check on sources of interference, etc. Nobody much liked the licence fees, although by 1930 more than 300,000 Canadians were paying their buck a year for the privilege of plucking sounds out of the air. In England that same year, the home licence fee was ten shillings; in India listeners were charged about $3.65 annually; and in Germany, better organized perhaps, licence fees were collected monthly and cost about 50 cents every 30 days.

But 1930 was already almost post-history in terms of the development of radio broadcasting in Canada. By then the country had 78 private, commercial radio stations, sixteen of them the so-called "phantom" stations which broadcast over the transmission facilities of more fully equipped stations. It had been 30 years since the immortal "one, two, three, four" had been sent by radio transmission through 50 miles of virgin North American air. And four years had passed since Ernie Bushnell, a pioneer of Canadian broadcasting, had inflicted the world's very first singing commercial on hapless Toronto area listeners. Written to the melody of "Three Blind Mice," the commercial extolled the virtues of the Toronto Wet Wash Laundry. It was an entirely appropriate harbinger of the laundry and detergent commercials which assaulted our senses for the rest of the century.

Most of the world credits Guglielmo Marconi with the invention of radio. Certainly he reaped the rewards, not least the assistance of the Canadian government in establishing his research facilities in Cape Breton at the beginning of the century. Marconi's most celebrated triumph was the transmission of a Morse radio signal from Cornwall, at the extreme tip of the British Isles, to a receiver on what has forever since been known as Signal Hill,

Signor Marconi observes while his assistants prepare to launch his antenna-carrying kite on Signal Hill. (Public Archives of Canada)

Guglielmo Marconi (facing camera, hand on bannister) was photographed on the steps of Cabot Tower on Signal Hill, St. John's, December 12, 1901. (Public Archives of Canada)

overlooking St. John's, Newfoundland. What the Italian inventor did on December 12, 1901, was to send the single letter "S" by Morse.

Neither Marconi, the rejoicing folk of Ottawa, nor the rest of the world had noticed that a year earlier, on December 23, 1900, a 36-year-old Canadian inventor had broadcast a total of 77 letters over a distance of about 50 miles. But Reginald Fessenden, the Sherbrooke boy who was chief chemist for both Thomas Edison and George Westinghouse before striking out on his own, wasn't sending Morse code; he was *talking* into a microphone. Speaking to his assistant at an experimental receiver in Arlington, Virginia, 50 miles from his Cobb Island laboratory, Fessenden said, "One, two, three, four. Is it snowing where you are, Mr. Thiessen? If so telegraph back and let me know."

George Westinghouse in a pensive moment. (Westinghouse Electric, Ltd.)

A close-up of Edison's recording device. (Thomas Alva Edison Foundation, Inc.)

Thomas Alva Edison with an early model of his cylinder recording machine. (Thomas Alva Edison Foundation, Inc.)

Moments later Fessenden's telegraph key rattled out Thiessen's message that it was, indeed, snowing at Arlington. The world's first radio broadcast of speech, of real sound as opposed to Morse signal, was a success.

An early portrait of Aubrey Reginald Fessenden. (CBC Archives)

Fessenden's transmitter and tower at Brant Rock, taken at the end of January, 1906. (North Carolina State Archives)

Fessenden (at right) with two of his assistants in the Brant Rock station and laboratory, 1906. (North Carolina State Archives)

Six years later, on December 24, 1906, Fessenden made the first public radio broadcast. He played "Oh Holy Night" on his violin, read the Christmas story from the New Testament, wished his listeners a Merry Christmas, and asked them to write if they had heard him. And they had. The mail response from incredulous radio operators on several ships lying off Boston proved the success of Fessenden's experiments.

Fessenden, a brilliant inventor who added the radio compass, the tracer bullet for machine guns and the first North American TV receiver (in 1919) to his accomplishments was not, however, a good businessman. Nor was he very successful in self-promotion. McGill University turned him down as a teacher of electrical engineering (they hired an American instead), and he had to turn to the U.S. Weather Bureau and to the United Fruit Company, which wanted better communication with its ships, for his funding. The Canadian government, which found $80,000 for Signor Marconi's work at Glace Bay, Nova Scotia, was equally unwilling to assist the Canadian. What the Ottawa mandarins did, instead, was to give the Italian Marconi initial exclusive rights to build any radio stations in Canada. So much for our inventor of "radio telephony," a man as much known today as the son of the lady who invented Empire Day in Canada.

There is clearly an element of poetic justice in the fact that although Signor Marconi's first radio station, XWA Montreal (now CFCF), was licenced and began broadcasting before any other station in North America, modern histories of radio, including those published in Canada, credit station KDKA Pittsburgh, a Johnny-come-lately, as being first. The actual chronology is as follows:

1905 Canada passed our first Wireless Telegraph

Act, intended to regulate and control Morse code radio broadcasts.

1913 The act was amended to include "radio-telephones" or "voice transmission."

1919 Donald Manson, a radio officer in the Royal Canadian Navy through World War I, was employed by the federal government as chief inspector of radio, and none too soon, because in September of that same year he was asked to issue a licence to Canada's (and North America's) first radio station.

1919 (September) Marconi radio station XWA was issued a licence to broadcast from its "factory" on William Street in Montreal.

1919 (December) XWA made its first broadcast, playing phonograph records over the air for the first time on this continent. (Fessenden's recital on Christmas Eve 14 years earlier was, you'll recall, a live performance.)

1920 (May 21) XWA broadcast its first regularly scheduled programme. The show included the contributions of a full orchestra and a Miss Dorothy Tulton as soloist. The audience included Prime Minister Sir Robert Borden, arctic explorer Vihljalmur Stefansson and William Lyon Mackenzie King (who would be prime minister, himself, just 19 months later). That splendid group, attending meetings of the Royal Society of Canada at the Chateau Laurier Hotel in Ottawa, heard the music from Marconi's Montreal transmitter over 100 miles distant, further than any previous-known broadcast.

1920 (November 2) KDKA Pittsburgh finally made it. With its first broadcast on this date, KDKA informed its listeners of Warren G. Harding's election as President of the United States, succeeding Woodrow Wilson.

From 1920 on, radio stations multiplied almost as quickly as the speak-easies and flappers of the jazz age. Canada's first commercial station, CJCB Winnipeg, owned by the *Winnipeg Free Press*, successor to the *Manitoba Free Press* established in 1872, broadcast a test programme in April, 1921 and began regular programming in July of that year. Still located in the Free Press Building on Winnipeg's Carlton Street, by 1980 the station was called CKRC, and was specializing in country and western music, a far cry from its salad days in the thirties and forties when it invited guests to a plush studio theatre for live programmes featuring a full studio orchestra and singers. That same year the Canadian National Railway broadcast band concerts from St. Catharines, Ontario, to receivers in a railway coach on the Canadian National Exhibition grounds in Toronto.

In 1923 the Canadian "firsts" began to multiply, almost to breed. In March alone, Canadians heard their first church broadcast (from Fort Rouge Methodist Church in Winnipeg); their first play-by-play hockey game (over CKCK Regina; the game, between Edmonton and Regina, was described by sportscaster Pete Parker); and their first university lecture (on the poetry of Bliss Carman, a Canadian who had, however, been living in Connecticut since 1908). Canada's public broadcasting was presaged, too, in 1923 with the inauguration of radio station CKY, operated through its telephone system by the Government of Manitoba.

In July the CNR added radio receivers to a parlour car out of Montreal, setting another precedent by broadcasting a message from President W. D. Robb to the captive audience before letting them hear some music. Three months later the railway company had radios in all of its parlour cars and was broadcasting news to them as well. The first

The photos were even more wooden than the performances: a chamber group preparing to broadcast over the CNR radio network. (Canadian National Railways Archives)

A CNR orchestra. Radio studios of the twenties were draped with cloth to prevent 'bouncy' sound, and the microphones were bigger than the bells of the saxophones. (Canadian National Railways Archives)

This publicity photo taken in the early twenties shows the drawing-room decor used in concert studios and the wall-to-wall drapes designed to keep the music muted and melodic. (Canadian National Railways Archives)

CNR *President W. D. Robb inaugurating the Montreal-Toronto train telephone service. (Public Archives of Canada)*

such broadcast was heard by British Prime Minister Lloyd George who was visiting Canada. He told the Canadian, American and British journalists toasting the inaugural newscast with him that it had been "invaluable" in informing him of world events "of the highest importance." None of this foreshadowed the brutal political warfare that occurred 40 years later when broadcast journalists began their efforts to invade the sacred precincts of federal and provincial legislatures, formerly open only to print reporters.

In 1924 the CNR opened its own radio station in the Chateau Laurier Hotel in Ottawa. That same

A CNR parlour car with radio and phonograph entertainment, all controlled by the railway 'operator' (back to the camera, upper right) who tuned the controls and adjusted the volume. (Canadian National Railways Archives)

year it broadcast Canada's first sponsored hockey game, a Stanley Cup contest between the Ottawa Senators and the Montreal Canadiens. The Senators are gone, but the radio station lingers on, still in the Chateau Laurier, as CBC station CBO. 1924 also heard the first Dominion Observatory time signals, broadcast from the facility at St. John, New Brunswick. The premiere livestock market reports were carried in January, 1925 on stations in Moncton, Winnipeg and Ottawa.

By now the CNR was up to its corporate larynx in transmitters, and in August Sir Henry Worth Thornton, the railway president, opened a station in Vancouver. In October the Canadian National made a broadcast from a moving train in Ontario, and on November 26, 1925 the BBC closed down in England so its listeners could hear a CNR programme beamed to them from Moncton.

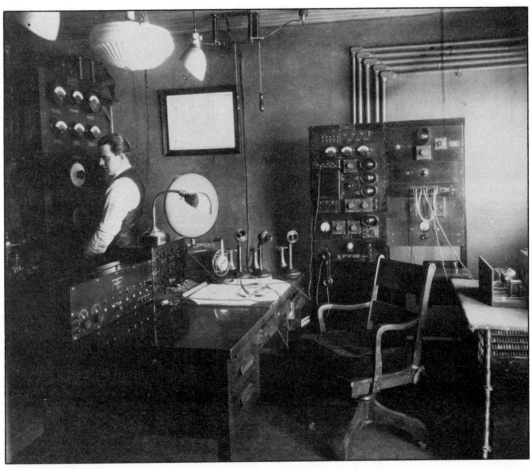

A CNR operating room for broadcast to the trains. Note the microphone beside the three telephones. (Canadian National Railways Archives)

But August had been the month for technical developments; that was when a Canadian company, Rogers, displayed the first radio receiver ever made which could be plugged into an electrical outlet in the home. The Rogers Batteryless (35 years before the world went portable crazy and began spreading sound pollution into every public area via transistor radios) was a mantel radio model and sold in the heady boom of the mid-twenties for $250. Oh, yes. The loudspeaker was an extra $45.

By 1926 there were only 15 radio sets in all of Canada's Yukon and Northwest Territories; but

RADIO AERIAL
ON OBSERVATION CAR

LISTENING - IN
ON OBSERVATION CAR

ALL
CANADIAN
NATIONAL
RAILWAYS
Through trains, are equipped with Radio receiving apparatus.

TEN
Broadcasting Stations extending Across
CANADA
FROM THE
ATLANTIC
TO THE
PACIFIC

CANADIAN NATIONAL RAILWAYS BROADCASTING STATION
AT MONCTON N.B.

BROADCASTING STUDIO
MONCTON N.B.

THE CANADIAN NATIONAL RAILWAYS
BROADCASTING STATION
OTTAWA CANADA

CNRO BROADCASTING STATION
OTTAWA ONT.

A photographic reproduction of a CNR ad from the twenties; the central picture shows the CN broadcast transmission towers at Moncton, New Brunswick. (Canadian National Railways Archives)

undeterred, arctic explorer Richard Byrd flew over the pole in a plane carrying a radio transmitter, just in case anyone was tuned in.

Regular school broadcasts began in October, 1927 from Vancouver, under supervision of that city's inspector of public schools. That same month Francophone Canadians heard transmissions in their native language, but from the CNR station in Edmonton, Alberta. The programme, like most

*A CNR operator at his
control station in a
railway parlour car.
(Canadian National
Railways Archives)*

subsequent French broadcasting outside Quebec,
was designed chiefly as an exercise in public
relations; the Canadian National on this occasion
in 1927 being anxious to promote a rail excursion
fare to Quebec.

1928 brought probably the first broadcast drama
produced in Canada onto the airwaves: CNRV
Vancouver presented three one-act plays by Vancouver authors. Eight months later in February of
1929, the CNRV Players, as they were known by
then, presented a complete version of Othello to
their listeners. Two months later, co-operating with
the Vancouver Shakespearian Society, they broadcast "The Merchant of Venice." The quality of
mercy for regional drama production became much
more strained after the CBC replaced the CNR as
Canada's major programmer. Despite an illustrious
history and a demonstrated skill, Vancouver
broadcasting has been vastly under-represented in
drama and variety productions across Canada.

In the early twenties, Vancouver studios lacked drapes and elaborate furniture, but not creative imagination. This tom-foolery was part of a CN station broadcast. (Canadian National Railways Archives)

The CBC has been unremitting in its devotion to its production facilities and staff in Toronto and Montreal. Even Vancouver's fancy new CBC production building was most obviously used in the seventies by visiting firemen from Toronto who produced shows like TV's "Ninety Minutes Live" on location, while Toronto production staffs were busily patronizing and irritating highly qualified "locals."

The year of the stock market crash also brought Canadian listeners regular classical music, broadcast live in the form of 25 concerts by the Toronto Symphony carried on the CNR national network. (The Metropolitan Opera premiered in Canada on Christmas Day, 1931 with "Hansel and Gretel.") 1929 was also the year that Canadians were driven close to lethal boredom by the initial broadcast of the series "The Nation's Business," a programme devoted to self-serving descriptions of governmental and political activity, delivered always in the most turgid prose which could be constructed. Other new traditions were to follow quickly. In 1932, for example, King George V was to make the first of those Christmas Day broadcasts from Buckingham Palace or Balmoral which still punctuate Christmas mornings throughout the Commonwealth.

But 1929 brought problems other than the incipient collapse of the speculator's bull market on Wall Street. Canada's broadcasting was virtually, like Topsy, without any organization or regulation; it had "just growed up." The CNR network aside, our 87 radio stations were a weird amalgam of private radio societies, commercial enterprises, and stations pumping out hate messages for the further glorification of rump evangelical societies and bible

◁The first microphones placed in the House of Commons were used during the Imperial Conference of 1932. In this photo, British Prime Minister Stanley Baldwin (standing, to the right of the Speaker's chair with its cluster of microphones) is addressing his colleagues. (Public Archives of Canada)

associations. Most distressing of all, especially to the proprietors of those stations, Canada was being engulfed by the much richer, higher-powered radio transmitters of New York, Chicago, Detroit, Seattle and the like. The 604 stations in the United States were swamping our airwaves, some even using the few frequencies agreed by the Canadian and American governments to be for the exclusive use of Canadian broadcasters.

So on December 6, 1928, Mackenzie King had appointed Sir John Aird, president of the Canadian Bank of Commerce, to head a royal commission enquiry "to examine into the broadcasting situation in the Dominion of Canada." Thus began the most unremitting chronicle of navel-gazing in the annals of recorded human society. There has scarcely been a year since without its royal commission, special study, parliamentary committee or public inquiry into broadcasting in Canada.

Unlike its successors, the Aird Commission worked quickly. It scheduled public hearings in 25 Canadian cities, listened to 164 oral presentations, waded through a further 124 written briefs, and presented its slim (and bilingual) 29-page report to the government on September 11, 1929. Sir John was given to a succinct expression of opinion, unlike those who followed him. He left no room for misunderstanding of his main conclusion, that the interests of the public "can be adequately served only by some form of public ownership, operation and control."

Nor did he mince words about the causal needs for a national, publicly owned broadcast service:

"At present the majority of programmes heard are from sources outside Canada. It has been emphasized to us that the continued reception of these has a tendency to mould the minds of the young people in the home to ideals and opinions

Sir John Aird, who had once owned a radio, but later "threw the damned thing out." (Canadian Imperial Bank of Commerce)

that are not Canadian. In a country of the vast geographical dimensions of Canada, broadcasting will undoubtedly become a great force in fostering a national spirit and interpreting national citizenship."

Quite an endorsement from the bank president who is quoted by broadcast pioneer T. J. Allard as having said shortly after his appointment to the royal commission that he'd "once owned a radio but later threw the damned thing out." Evidently untroubled, however, by his personal distaste for the impertinent, young medium, Sir John Aird pressed his study home — and abroad. Having visited London, Berlin, Paris, Brussels, the Hague, Geneva, Dublin, Belfast and New York (where there may have been some cultural compensations), the commission also toured most of Canada and observed:

"We are of the opinion that the development of broadcasting *far beyond its present state, and this may include television* (author's emphasis) is one of great importance and should be kept pace with so that the service in Canada would continue equal to that in any other country."

The commission also noted that in its hearings and briefs, "there has been unanimity on one fundamental question — Canadian radio listeners want Canadian broadcasting."

What Sir John and his colleagues did not know was that there was a federal election in the country's future, and that Prime Minister Mackenzie King who had appointed them was about to be defeated by Conservative R. B. Bennett. So the commission's urging for the establishment of a "Canadian Radio Broadcasting Company," to be funded by licence fees on receivers, "rental of time...for indirect advertising," and a small federal subsidy was put aside. It wasn't until 1933 that a beleaguered federal Conservative government under Prime Minister Bennett took the microphone in its teeth, as it were, and created what it called "The Canadian Radio Broadcasting Commission." It has gone mostly unnoted since then that the precursor of the CBC had its beginnings that year on April Fool's Day. Not every subsequent act of the Canadian Broadcasting Corporation has denied its natal origins.

Public Trough Versus Private Profit: 1929-1932

Until the end of the 1920's, revenues from radio broadcasting had been mostly as flat as a flapper's bosom. Early radio stations, in Canada as in the United States, had three major categories of operation: one was public relations for a particular view of the bible or for a corporation such as the CNR; a second was programming by companies such as RCA, Marconi or Northern Electric, designed to make radio receiver sales more attractive; a third was the operation of early stations by private "radio clubs" formed because radio receivers had no value for listeners unless there was programming.

In Canada commercials were banned before 1925. Even the United States prohibited commercial messages in the early twenties. The purpose of radio stations in the United States in that period was, quite simply, to sell radios, a notion conceived by David Sarnoff. In 1912 he was a 22-year-old telegrapher who translated the names of survivors of the Titanic tragedy from Morse code, and telegraphed them from his radio room in a New York department store. By 1919 he was president of RCA, a stepping stone to enormous power in the American broadcasting industry.

By 1926 in Canada nine of the existing radio stations were owned by newspapers; twenty-three were operated by amateur (radio club) groups; ten more were owned by radio receiver manufacturers, and others by the CNR, by the University of Alberta,

David Sarnoff received and transcribed the names of survivors from the Titanic in his telegraphy room in Wanamaker's Department Store in New York City. (Broadcast Pioneers' Library, Washington, D.C.)

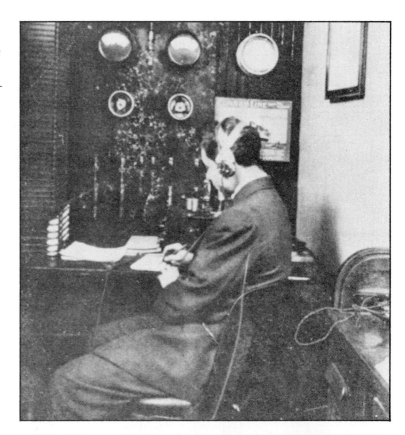

A sophisticated, battery-powered radio receiver, circa 1924; this one, horn speaker and all, was in use in the Northwest Territories, at Chesterfield Inlet, when photographed. No earphones needed here, as with crystal sets, and the community was probably too remote for the federal licence fee collectors. (Public Archives of Canada)

1926: a studio built for the Jehovah's Witness Edmonton radio station, CHCY, *in the home of a church member. (Private collection: Beryl White)*

The transmission tower for station CHCY *(Private collection: Beryl White)*

Queen's University, and by the Government of
Manitoba. So far advertising had mostly consisted
of the indirect form recommended by the Aird
Commission — just a brief announcement at the
beginning or end of a programme stating that
such-and-so a company had provided the funding
for the broadcast.

In the United States, where broadcasting was
largely unregulated, there was one critical rule:
recorded material could not be used. So, although
many musicians were content to perform for
nothing, the problem of filling air time became

*Toronto bible station
CKCX was located in
this Scarborough
home. (Private collec-
tion: Frank Wain-
wright)*

*The Jehovah's Wit-
ness radio studios on
Inkerman Street in To-
ronto, 1929. (Private
collection: Alex Deach-
man)*

crucial. But when the prohibition against commercials was lifted, American stations were quickly earning substantial revenues from sponsors, and bombarding Canadians with live entertainment of substantially greater interest than the mostly recorded broadcasts carried in Canada. By the end of the twenties, it was estimated that 80 per cent of Canadians were listening to American stations at any given time.

Moreover, given their advertising revenue, the American stations were able to build bigger and stronger radio transmitters. American stations were booming across the border with transmitters powered up to 50,000 watts, often completely covering and blanketing the signals of Canadian stations hundreds of miles closer to Canadian listeners. Meanwhile, most Canadian radio stations were operating on only 1,000 watts of power, and often on much less. (In 1954 an announcer at CKRD Red Deer, Alberta, reflecting that his station's transmitting power of 250 watts was less than that of a tri-light lamp, got himself fired for telling a breathless audience that "you are listening to CKRD Red Deer, your central Alberta light bulb.") American stations, briefly, were easier to hear and usually more interesting.

One Canadian station, Toronto's CFRB, had already broken ground for the massive Canadian purchases of American TV programmes by joining the Columbia Broadcasting Service in 1929 and carrying American network broadcasts. Another Toronto area station, owned by a distillery, Gooderham & Worts, Ltd., became a member of the NBC's red network. The distillery-owned station, CKGW, came into being when the Liberal government under Mackenzie King decided, in 1928, to re-allocate broadcasting frequencies as a means of shutting down several bible society stations which were broadcasting

In 1929 radio station CFRB had its transmitter at Aurora, Ontario. (Public Archives of Canada)

brutal hate messages about every belief other than their own. A sample script: "The Roman Catholic hierarchy has begun and carries on its assaults against God's true people. In every country of earth the hierarchy carries forward this wicked persecution." Stations were being operated by the national bible students' association of the Jehovah's Witnesses as well as by the Jarvis Street Baptist Church in Toronto and even a Roman Catholic cathedral, St. Michael's.

But in gerrymandering the pentecostals off the airwaves the government left itself open, especially after the opening of CKGW, to charges it preferred "booze over the bible." The provocation had doubtless been great. In Saskatchewan, for example, a

Proprietors of the fundamentalist radio stations were infuriated by Prime Minister Mackenzie King's efforts to shut them down. This advertisement for a public protest meeting appeared in the Toronto Globe *in 1928.*

Who Owns the Air?

By their recent drastic action in refusing to renew the licenses of the International Bible Students' Association, the Dominion Government has denied them the use of the air as a means of preaching the Word of God to the people.

Why did they not deny this privilege to all denominations?

On Sunday last, in the city of Toronto, where one of the Bible Students' radio stations is located, services were broadcast from the Roman Catholic church, the Jewish synagogue, the Anglican church, the Baptist church, and the United church, but the International Bible Students' Association was refused the same privilege.

Though some may disagree with the teachings of this Association, many thousands embrace them, and are receiving benefit and good therefrom. These are seeking to know why they are suddenly deprived of the opportunity of hearing these programs over the air.

Hundreds of thousands of people have signified their disapproval of the Government's action by signing petitions asking the Government to ignore the protests of a few and to permit the Association's program to be broadcast. Thus far the Government has not heeded this request.

Why This Silence When the Rights of the People Are Endangered?

WHY THIS DISCRIMINATION AGAINST THE INTERNATIONAL BIBLE STUDENTS' ASSOCIATON?

FREEDOM OF SPEECH AND RELGIOUS TOLERANCE ARE IN DANGER!

Are you in favor of freedom for the people? Do you believe in British fair play? Then attend the

Mass Meeting

Pantages Theater, Sunday, April 15, 7.30 p.m.

Organ Recital at 7 o'Clock

Addresses by A. L. Deachman, of Toronto, and other prominent speakers.

Doors Open 6.45.   Seats Free.   No Collection.

bible station had gone commercial and rented time to the Ku Klux Klan! It was in this atmosphere that Prime Minister King, selecting the high road to compromise and political whitewash, chose and appointed Canada's first royal commission on broadcasting, the Aird Commission.

The Aird Commission recommendations were warmly received by most Canadians. They included: establishment of seven 50-thousand watt radio transmitters across the country; control of all broadcasting by federal government with no commercial content; an increase in the radio licence fee to $3.00 yearly; and provisions that "there should be regulations prohibiting statements of a controversial nature or one religion making an attack upon the leaders or doctrine of another ... that the broadcasting of political matters should be carefully restricted," and for the employment of "competent and cultured announcers only." Except for the *Toronto Globe*, which decried "civil service broadcasting," Canadian newspapers supported the commission.

But the summer election of 1930 intervened, and the R. B. Bennett government, returned to office, found itself faced with two brand new lobbies. On one side were the badly organized and disparate commercial radio stations calling themselves the Canadian Broadcasters' Association. Their chief spokesman was Ernie Bushnell, then manager of CKNC Toronto, later assistant general manager and then vice-president of CBC before carving a private broadcasting empire of his own.

On the other side was Graham Spry, a former Rhodes Scholar and now in 1930 national secretary of the Association of Canadian Clubs. One month after Prime Minister Bennett met his first parliament in September, 1930, Graham Spry and a colleague, lumber heir Alan Plaunt, another Oxonian, formed the Radio League of Canada. Using a well-coordinated "old boy" network, Spry and Plaunt rapidly enlisted the support of a half dozen provincial superintendents of education, a dozen university presidents, womens' organizations with an aggregate membership of 600,000, and 50 newspapers with a combined circulation of over one million — all of them dedicated to the Radio League of Canada's goal of nationalized radio directed through a public corporation with no commercial advertising of any kind.

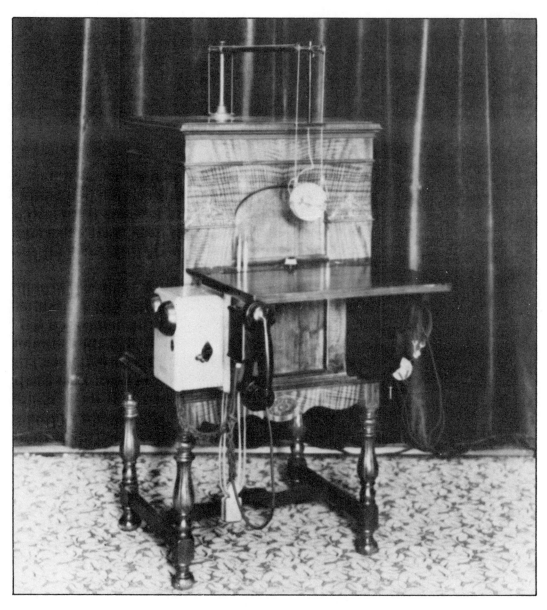

The Toronto Globe, *which broadcast three newscasts daily over* CFRB, *had a perceived vested interest in avoiding the competition of "civil service broadcasting." This is the equipment used for the Globe's newscasts. (Public Archives of Canada)*

Graham Spry, not content to work the 'old boys'' network, often took to the public stump to promote his vision of publicly owned and controlled broadcasting. (Public Archives of Canada)

The newspaper support for the RLC was scarcely surprising. The publishers were terrified that a spread of commercial radio would bite hugely into *their* advertising dollars. Canadian politicians, having had as yet no access to the airwaves (in the United States, Presidents Harding and Coolidge had made a few "radio talks"), were naturally anxious to avoid alienating the news barons whom they saw as their most powerful potential allies — or enemies.

It was only radio, but appearances must be maintained, even in this 1933 Halifax studio. (CBC Archives)

This room in the Royal York Hotel, Toronto, was specially decorated and equipped to serve as a concert studio. (Public Archives of Canada)

The struggle between public and private broadcast supporters wasn't the only one initiated with the decade of the thirties. While that war was being waged across the country, directed mostly from the plush parlours of Ottawa's Rideau Club, another was going on in the courts. Several provinces, led by Quebec, wanted control of broadcasting in their own provinces, free of federal interference. Through most of 1931, in the Supreme Court of Canada and at the Privy Council in London, England (then Canada's court of last resort), there was a no-holds battle between Quebec and Ottawa over jurisdiction in broadcasting. When the Supreme Court ruled in Ottawa's favour in a three-to-two decision, Premier Taschereau of Quebec moved the proceedings to London, only to be defeated again. Thus confirmed

Quebec Premier A. Taschereau spear-headed the losing battle to wrest control of broadcasting from Ottawa with eloquent and fiery speeches. (Public Archives of Canada)

On March 13, 1931, Prime Minister R. B. Bennett (flanked here by his full cabinet) spoke with Sir George Perley over a trans-Atlantic telephone hook-up. Bennett was in Ottawa, Sir George in Buenos Aires, Argentina. (Public Archives of Canada)

in a supreme federal jurisdiction in broadcasting, Prime Minister Bennett immediately established a parliamentary committee, the first of many, "to advise and recommend a complete technical scheme of broadcasting for Canada."

Spry and his colleagues urged formation of a Canadian broadcasting corporation cast in the likeness of the BBC. The Canadian Broadcasters' Association, led by Ernie Bushnell, asked for subsidy of national network programming and for the extension of services to sparsely settled areas, but wanted to maintain the status quo with regard to the regulation and operation of private and commercial stations.

When the smoke had cleared from the parliamentary committee rooms early in 1932, Bennett was ready. On May 16 he introduced a bill to the House of Commons establishing a public, national broadcasting system. On May 26 the legislation creating the Canadian Radio Broadcasting Commission was given royal assent.

The new creature thus ordained was born a cripple, the incomplete child of a classic Canadian compromise. Against the advice of the Radio League, the commission was given no government subsidies

The Canadian Radio Broadcasting Commission appointed in 1932 comprised, from left to right, Thomas Maher, Lt. Colonel Arthur Steel, Colonel R. Landry and Hector Charlesworth. (CBC Archives)

and was not set up as a corporation; its employees were civil servants. The commission, headed by a three-man board, was given the revenue from a licence fee raised from $2.00 to $3.00. It was to establish a national programme service and, at the same time, regulate private broadcasting in Canada.

The first commissioners — a magazine editor, a forestry engineer, and a second engineer from the Department of National Defence — set about acquiring the CNR's stations and building a network. But their Canadian listeners were already hooked on American programmes with Amos and Andy, Rudy Vallee, Fred Allen, and Jack Armstrong, the all-American boy, not to mention, ironically, Canadian bandleader Guy Lombardo.

The super-sensitive radio transmission tubes had even changed a whole style of music: because the equipment in early radio stations tended to blow out when assaulted by high musical notes, singers were asked to keep it soft when warbling into the lampshades that usually hid their microphones, protecting them from "mike fright." The lady who followed those instructions best, Vaughn de Leath, thereby invented in 1920 a style that came to be known as "crooning." Her first and

*Vaughn de Leath,
who invented croon-
ing, had the heft to
handle the king-sized
microphones of the
early twenties.
(Broadcast Pioneers'
Library, Washington,
D.C.)*

most illustrious student and beneficiary was Bing Crosby.

The Canadian Radio Broadcasting Commission managed to get on the air in 1933 using equipment borrowed from the CNR, but its operations from then until the end of 1935 were sloppy, *ad hoc*, and disorganized. That year, 1935, brought the first federal election campaign since the establishment of the commission and, subsequently, its death of an ostentatiously self-inflicted wound.

The CBC and the Dawn of Empire: 1932-1936

The years between establishment of the Canadian Radio Broadcasting Commission and 1935 were not uneventful. On November 26, 1934, just two years after the commission was appointed, a newly graduated electrical engineer from McGill University, Alphonse Ouimet, joined the CRBC after a brief, two-year experience with the experimental Canadian Television Company in Montreal. Ouimet, applying the engineering notion that creative personnel were as interchangeable as cathode tubes and fuses, was to come closer than anyone to utterly destroying the CBC from the president's office 32 years later.

Late in 1933 Ernie Bushnell, inventor of the singing commercial, was hired as programme director of the CRBC, replacing E. A. Weir, who had been the first programming boss of the public network. Weir, who had headed the CNR's radio services, had run afoul of the first of many internal political battles within the network, and depressed by the death of his wife in childbirth, had left the CRBC in November, 1933. Bushnell, then as ever irrepressible, was to stay with the CRBC, soon to be the CBC, for 26 years.

But 1935 was the big year. In that year, CRBC listeners were treated to a full day of broadcasts honouring the silver jubilee of King George V. They heard a dramatization of the founding of Empire Day in Canada; they were given a broadcast relayed

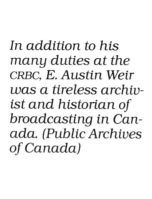

In addition to his many duties at the CRBC, E. Austin Weir was a tireless archivist and historian of broadcasting in Canada. (Public Archives of Canada)

from the United States of funeral services for Will Rogers; and in July they heard live the sounds of Mount Vesuvius as captured by a microphone held over the rim of that infamous crater. Via radio Canada also witnessed its first skirmish in the bilingual and bicultural battle. French language announcements used occasionally on the CRBC stations were denounced, chiefly by western editorialists, as "unconstitutional" and part of "a concerted effort by people of French origin to make Canada a bilingual country."

1935 also saw the introduction from Banff, Alberta of the sort of petty broadcast dishonesty that has since become a hallmark of CBC radio and television. Scheduled to participate in the "Canada Celebrates Christmas" broadcast, local station manager "Tiny" Elphicke was frustrated by the late arrival of the transcontinental railway train, which he was to broadcast live. So he rounded up a group of locals, persuaded the railway to shunt a yard engine up to his microphones, and directed the town's residents to shout greetings to the de-training "passengers" on his "live" Christmas broadcast. Nowadays, deception is taken as read by listeners accustomed, for example, to melifluous announcements on CBC radio's "As It Happens" that "so-and-so is standing by in London," when they know perfectly well that so-and-so was tape-recorded several hours earlier. Ironically, the Americans, regarded as commercial shills by many Canadian broadcasters, are required to state when programme material is recorded, while for their Canadian critics, such cheap and shabby deceptions are only the small change of ethical whoredom, unnoticed by most and unremarked by the rest.

But it was in political broadcasting that the Canadian Radio Broadcasting Commission found the lever for its own destruction. Canadian politicians had no special anxieties about deceiving the public, so long as it was even-handed. What they could not abide was unnatural advantage.

Which brings us to the broadcasts between September 24 and October 5, 1935, of the "Uncle Sage" radio series during that year's federal election campaign. A brainchild of the J. J. Gibbons advertising agency, the programmes featured actor Robert Lucas as a folksy Cassandra who, in dramatized conversations, told the Canadian electorate what rapscallions and scoundrels the Liberals really were. Uncle Sage created consternation in the ranks of the Liberals in the wake of the Beauharnois hydro scandal (which he mentioned in lip-licking detail), and they demanded that the sponsor be identified on further broadcasts. And so he was — as one R. L. Wright, an employee, as it turned out, of the Conservative ad agency. The Conservative Party of Canada's skirts were thereby kept clean.

Unhappily for the Tories, for Uncle Sage and for the Gibbons agency, the Liberals won the 1935 election. Furious with the attacks on his party and policies, the new and once-again Prime Minister Mackenzie King convened a special parliamentary committee on broadcasting (already our third). The committee presented its third and final report on May 26, 1936, recommending abolition of the CRBC and establishment in its place of a crown corporation which was to be the CBC. The committee report, from a majority membership of Liberal MP's, also noted that:

"During the last election year there was a serious abuse of broadcasting for political purposes and that lack of a proper control by the commission was apparent. The most glaring instance brought before the committee was related to the "Uncle Sage" broadcasts, in which offensive personal references were frequent and to which no proper or adequate political sponsorship was given. Some of these offensive broadcasts originated in the Toronto studios of the Radio Commission."

Even worse in the view of Canadian MP's and the Scottish bankers who were busily building the new temples of twentieth-century Canadian culture, some of the programmes had been produced on credit: "We also find that credit was issued to political parties in direct violation of the rules of the commission." Ever since 1935 political parties and candidates have found it virtually impossible to buy radio and TV time without payment in advance.

The committee's subsequent recommendations were pointed, succinct, and since 1935 have been accorded the status of Holy Writ. They were four:
1) That dramatized political broadcasts be prohibited.
2) That full sponsorship of all political broadcasts be required.
3) That the limitation and distribution of time for political broadcasts be under the complete control of the Corporation (the CBC).
4) That no political broadcasts be allowed on election day or during two days immediately preceding same.

This last recommendation was the first of many left-handed compliments to the impact of broadcast journalism which, unlike print media, is assumed capable of warping voters' minds at the penultimate electoral moment. Newspapers were allowed, then as now, to carry advertising, editorial exhortation and news columns on election campaigns up to and including election day itself.

Mackenzie King had his vindication and his revenge. When parliament reconvened in September, 1936 after the summer recess, he told it that a new public broadcast service and authority (the CBC) would be put in place later in the year. On November 2, 1936 the Canadian Broadcasting Corporation was born. The fledgling had at least one of the fatal flaws of its predecessor, the Canadian Radio Broadcasting Commission. Like the CRBC, the CBC was to be both principal and participant, both player and referee of Canadian radio. The CBC, to its pain and ultimately its chagrin, was to continue to be the regulatory *and* licencing agent for Canadian broadcasting.

In yet another harbinger of a continuing CBC predilection for tunnel vision, the corporation selected as general manager a man who was a public relations specialist, not a programmer, and whose radio career had proceeded, not in Canada, but in England. He was, however, a Canadian born. Major W. E. Gladstone Murray, former director of public relations for the BBC, provided the first graphic demonstration of the homily that Canadian birth was no bar to success in Canadian broadcasting if one first earned a reputation abroad.

Despite the political/partisan gaffes of the CRBC, radio had progressed with some alacrity during the late twenties and early thirties. In December, 1930 British stage director Tyrone Guthrie had arrived in Montreal to direct a series of historical Canadian radio dramas titled "The Romance of Canada" for the CNR broadcast service. His return decades later as founder and guru of the Stratford Festival was to be more auspicious and more lasting in its impact.

Gladstone Murray is flanked in this picture by Lorne Greene (left) and Ernie Bushnell. (Public Archives of Canada)

When Tyrone Guthrie arrived in Canada in December, 1930 to produce "The Romance of Canada" series, he was the very model of a twenties romantic lead. (E. A. Weir Collection: Public Archives of Canada)

Besides offering network radio listeners such treats as a 1,000-voice children's choir and the sound of "O Canada" played on the Peace Tower carillon from Ottawa (on Canada's Diamond Jubilee, July 1, 1927), the CNR also provided one of the most egregious examples of bad taste in broadcast history with the introduction from Vancouver of "The Four Porters." At that time, as for many years to come, it was an ironclad CNR policy that only blacks were employed as porters and only whites got the more prestigious and higher-paying work as conductors

The Four Porters, pho-
tographed in Van-
couver's CNRV in 1925.
(Public Archives of
Canada)

on the company's trains. But The Four Porters, a singing group who added piano and saxophone to racial insult, were *whites* who performed, in studio, in porters' jackets, porters' caps and blackface make-up!

Ironically, in the early fifties, because of the peculiarities of the first television cameras, *all* white performers were required to wear *coloured* make-up, most often in bilious shades of garish green. Even into the sixties TV cameras and studio lights continued to require elaborate deception to proximate an appearance of reality. Newscasters and politicians quickly learned that on home sets white shirts looked as though they were grey. So everyone wore pale blue or grey shirts which, on TV, came out looking sparkly white. You can understand the irony implicit in that technical reversal of reality when you recall those legions of ladies pawing through two piles of washing during laundry commercials in the fifties and sixties and exclaiming brightly, "This pile is much whiter! You can see the difference. Those look grey. I'm going to use this soap from now on."

There must have been a considerable attrition of spontaneity given that the clothes that looked whiter had to be treated before shooting those commercials to make them literally grey so they would photograph as white, and vice-versa with the other stack of laundry which looked grey.

Thus were the soap hucksters encouraged in their confidence in the efficacy of deception by the electronic requirements of their new, video playpens.

Private radio, though characterized chiefly by its disarray, was also showing some evidence of the economic muscle it was to flex in the second half of the century. In 1931 at the beginning of the Great Depression, Roy Thompson, a gent who was to complain 35 years later that he was well shy of his financial goal, as he was still short by $250 million of his billion-dollar target, grossed an $80,000 income through a radio station in North Bay, Ontario. And all of that with an obsolete transmitter apparatus which Thompson and his brother-in-law humped into the trunk of their beat-up car after persuading Ernie Bushnell in Toronto to sell it to them for a promissary note of $500. Adding insult to impertinence, Thompson hired the CKNC engineer whom Bushnell sent to North Bay to put the "box" in working order at $25 weekly, a $20 cut from his salary in Toronto, and further hustled Bushnell to lend him $160 for two transmitter tubes which Northern Electric refused to supply on Thompson's already deflated credit.

Thompson, who had just come through bankruptcy proceedings, was later to own and control

This was, in the winter of 1923, the entire studio facility of CKNC. The equipment shown is probably the same gear later discarded, and bought in 1931 by Roy Thompson. (Public Archives of Canada)

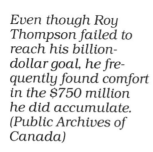

Even though Roy Thompson failed to reach his billion-dollar goal, he frequently found comfort in the $750 million he did accumulate. (Public Archives of Canada)

one of the largest publishing and broadcasting empires in the world as Lord Thompson of Fleet. He is best known for his gloating comment, on receipt of his first TV broadcast licence, that it was "like a licence to print money." Thompson's purchase of the staid *Times* of London and the *Sunday Times* was his entrance fee to proper society in Britain, where he made his final home. But it was from his proliferation of small newspapers and radio and TV stations that he built the $750 million that later dissatisfied him so profoundly. The "dirty thirties" saw the beginnings of two broadcast dynasties: that of Lord Thompson of Fleet, and the CBC. Both, eventually, developed the constituency they deserved.

It was no great surprise to members of the Radio League of Canada, headed by Graham Spry, that Mackenzie King's legislation created a public broadcasting system very like the one they had been advocating since 1931. Spry had played Canada's "old boy" network like a virtuoso throughout the existence of the league. Its first meeting in Alan Plaunt's Ottawa home had been attended, for example, by Gordon Robertson (then and for another 40 years Canada's indisputably most powerful bureaucratic mandarin), and by Jack W. Pickersgill (Mackenzie King's secretary, later a trusted cabinet colleague, and later still official trustee and editor of the voluminous King diaries). Building on a chain of relationships dating to student days at McGill and at Oxford, the league's supporters even took care to woo Francophone support, suggesting to French-language newspaper publishers that they editorialize against the dangers of blanket American invasion of Quebec's airwaves in the absence of a national broadcast service.

Although Radio League supporters had common goals, their motives were a mixed bag. For instance, their legal counsel was an ambitious Montreal lawyer, Brooke Claxton, who was later (in 1943) Mackenzie King's assistant as president to the (privy) council, and later still federal minister of health and welfare (1944) and minister of national defence (1947). Said Claxton in a 1930 letter to Graham Spry:

"As you know, I have no radio and have never listened to radio if I could possibly avoid it. I am really keen to have the programs given to the

Brooke Claxton on the campaign trail during the 1949 general election campaign. (Public Archives of Canada)

Canadian people *made as bad as possible, in order that radio may pass out. For that reason alone I am in favour of government control."* (author's emphasis)

It was with such sublime confidence in public broadcasting that the Radio League played midwife to the CBC. And it was through the comments of men like Aird and Claxton that generations of radio and television producers, writers and performers came to have less than absolute faith in the loyalty, understanding and support of their political and bureaucratic masters.

The Magic Years: 1935-1939

The decade from 1935 to 1945 was the magic era in radio. Taking a lead from Busby Berkeley and all the other producers of escapist movies — from the Hollywood musical spectacles Berkeley raised to an art form and the biblical epics that brought Cecil B. De Mille wealth and fame (while De Mille was busy rewriting Canadian history in a series of appalling films about the Riel Rebellion and the RCMP) — radio helped us put the "dirty thirties" aside for a few moments or hours of fantasy and delight.

Never mind the "Bennett buggy" outside the prairie shack, the car now horse-drawn because no one could afford repairs in the last days of Bennett's government. Never mind the empty belly or the single light bulb unscrewed and carried from one room to another (in those houses blessed by electricity). The crystal set or the genuine wood console radio, probably a Rogers Majestic, made all the world accessible and exciting. The bailiff stopped work at 6 p.m., and with the doors safely shut against the outer darkness and the world of bread lines, repossessions, hardship and grinding frustration, everyone could enjoy a holiday from impotence with Amos and Andy, Fred Allen, Jack Benny, Eddy Cantor and the rest. There might be a dust garden outside the kitchen door, but "Lux Radio Theatre" was waiting, with Paulette Goddard or Douglas Fairbanks there to whisk you to Araby, the China Sea or the high mountains of Tibet.

Something else was going on, along with the entertainment, the flight from reality and the conviction that purchase of the right soap could make life more glamourous. There was a social revolution underway. It had begun with the "broadsheets" that preceded our first newspapers, and now radio was making information available even to the illiterate, to people who had no access to daily newspapers or were able to read them only with puzzled and pained difficulty. The elite in society had long known that information was power; their working knowledge of that equation provided their strong grip on society's levers.

But now, without anyone having planned it, the power base was shifting and broadening. By the time the CBC came into being on April 1, 1935, it was already certain that the public would become sceptical of our major social institutions; voters would begin to perceive that even good politicians tell lies; and eventually a major war (Viet Nam) would end in defeat, support for it withdrawn by a U.S. television audience sickened by its excesses. Moreover, two Canadian prime ministers (Louis St. Laurent and Pierre Trudeau) and a pair of American presidents (Lyndon Johnson and Richard Nixon) would be forced from office by voter indignation — all based on perceptions gained chiefly from the broadcast media.

By 1935 broadcasting had become integral to western society. And society would never be the same again. When those cheerful folk on the red network and the blue network (organized by NBC in 1928) said, "eat me" and "drink me," we did. Neither they nor their listeners knew that the elixir of wider knowledge would soon make us grow, like Alice following those same instructions, until we began bursting through the stringent

Foster Hewitt, seen here in 1958 with CBC producer Thom Benson (left) and ex-Maple Leaf star Sid Smith. (CBC Archives)

confines of our social/political imprisonment — an arm sticking out here, a head there.

Play-by-play hockey broadcasts were already old hat by 1935. Canada's first broadcast, from the Toronto arena, was made on February 8, 1923 by Norman Albert. Like Fessenden, nobody remembers him, either. But Foster Hewitt, already a successful sportswriter and announcer, made *his* first hockey broadcast on March 22 of that year, and by the time Hewitt got around to shouting, "He shoots! He scores!" for the first time, *everybody* knew him. By 1935 there was probably no small Canadian boy within reach of a radio who wasn't listening to Hewitt and saving Beehive Corn Syrup labels, in return for which he could get, by mail, pictures of King Clancy, Lionel (Big Train) Conacher and the other NHL immortals.

Almost 60 years after its primitive beginnings, the hockey broadcast is still the biggest audience attraction in Canada. The only substantive difference today, with hockey being broadcast on television, is that sportscasters can no longer simulate exciting play by shouting into their microphones as they did during a radio broadcast. Since people can now *see* dull play, violence has been added, a technique borrowed from the hugely popular wrestling of television's early days. There is nothing like the thunder of bodies careening into the boards, heads and helmets cracking the ice — all faithfully captured by high-technology shotgun mikes — to add zest to the game. By adding violence, the NHL's moguls have adapted to the real politique of television.

Drama in the early thirties was mostly the preserve of private radio. In Vancouver Fletcher Markle and Alan Young were learning a trade which would later take both to Hollywood. Their gifted acting colleague, John Drainie, was to become one of Canada's most respected performers. In Winnipeg Tommy Tweed was writing and producing radio dramas, as well as acting in them for the few extra dollars, and Esse Ljungh, later one of Canada's finest radio drama directors and producers, was running classes for aspiring actors. In Toronto at CFRB, Andrew Allan, who would become, with Ljungh, the other half of the CBC's formidable drama department in the forties and fifties, was working with Robert Christie and a host of other performers, most of whom acted on radio for no payment beyond the exposure and the experience.

But the first radio drama to rivet all of North America's attention was the real thing. It came on April 12, 1936 from the improbable location of a small gold mine in Nova Scotia, and was transmitted from an old-fashioned wall telephone by a young

Fletcher Markle (CBC Archives)

Esse Ljungh at the director's intercom; he accepted nothing less than total concentration. (CBC Archives)

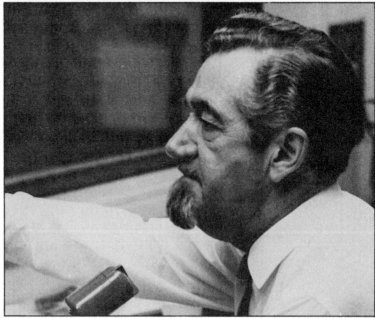

CBC announcer, J. Frank Willis. The Moose River disaster, which Willis described in five-minute bulletins every half hour for 111 hours, was carried on every one of Canada's 58 radio stations, and by 650 radio stations in the United States affiliated with the Mutual, Columbia and National broadcasting networks. Frank Willis had to do battle with a phalanx of newspaper reporters for the only telephone line in the tiny community, as he waited out the ordeal of three men trapped 141 feet below

John Drainie at work. He was the compleat professional — every performance given everything he had, every reading a lesson for his peers. (Private collection: Bronwyn Drainie)

An early photo of Andrew Allan (in the suit) with maestro Lucio Agostini. Producers in early CBC radio had many duties; note the sign: "No smoking ... It is the responsibility of the producer to see that this regulation is enforced." (Public Archives of Canada)

the minehead. Two were rescued before he ended his marathon series of broadcasts. Thirteen months later, on May 6, 1937, listeners heard the unprofessional, but admirably human sobs of another radio commentator, as blazing bodies spilled from the Hindenburg, burning and crumpling above the dirigible mooring at Lakehurst, New Jersey.

Audience ratings were primitive at best in the thirties. (Many say they still are.) It was one of the earliest surveys in Chicago in 1936 which gave us the relentless myth that audiences have an average education of grade six and the mentality of a 12-year-old. Of course grade six education was probably a fair average in a city wracked for seven

J. Frank Willis at
Moose River, April
1936: endurance with
grace. (CBC Archives)

Frank Willis main-
tained his individual-
ity even when the ex-
igencies of his trade
required him to don a
flying suit to board an
early thirties biplane;
note the diamond
socks. (CBC Archives)

years by the Great Depression and swollen with tens of thousands of illiterate migrant workers from sharecropping land in the deep south. But the lowest-common-denominator theory persisted for decades, although the reality was somewhat different in the fifties and sixties when ad agencies were producing television commercials still aimed at the same, legendary "average" viewer.

If programme ratings had been taken in Canada, they'd have doubtless placed "The Happy Gang" right behind "Hockey Night In Canada." Bert Pearl's troupe of highly skilled professional musicians laughed and played their way into Canadian homes and hearts from 1937 until 1957, when radio's omnivorous baby brother, television, began starving the senior service of budgets and creative talent. But the nostalgia and the yearning for those palmier days lived on. As late as 1976 I was told by the producer of CBC's flagship morning radio show, "Next season I want this program to be like the Happy Gang, to earn and hold the attention and affection of a really loyal, committed audience."

By 1937, too, CBC had actually gotten around to appointing a head of drama, who then, of course, had to invent a department for himself. His name was Rupert Lucas and he began by hiring Charles Warburton of New York to produce 11 Shakespearian dramas, beginning in October, 1938. The stars included such notables as Sir Cedric Hardwicke and Walter Huston.

It is still true, 45 years later, that American and British credentials open employment doors faster at any Canadian TV network than does domestic experience. A good many Canadians, acutely aware of this soft spot in the Canadian psyche, have gone to the United States or Britain for the credits they need to start at the top in Canada. A few have returned. Some, like Bernie Braden, who began

Clowning it up for CBC public relations cameras are "Happy Gang" regulars Bob Farnon (left), Kathleen Stokes, Blaine Mathe and Bert Pearl (at piano). (CBC Archives)

with Alan Young and Juliette in Vancouver in 1940, and who returned abortively to star for the fledgling Global TV network, have found no fatted calves. Others, like Fletcher Markle, came back to find themselves surrounded by the poisonous envy of colleagues who resented their experience in feature film production in Hollywood. A few, like Daryl Duke and Joyce Davidson, have managed by commuting between New York and Toronto, or Los Angeles and Vancouver. Individual producers and directors employed by a programme series have fared better; they are almost always certain of a comfortable CBC sinecure if, for example, they have even the most tenuous of BBC experiences in their recent history. All of this in a direct line of descent from W. Gladstone Murray, a senior officer of the BBC in the later twenties who was invited to the founding meeting of Graham Spry's Radio League in 1930, and later became general manager of the CBC.

Whatever its failings and tentative beginnings, radio had become close to ubiquitous before World War II. Weather forecasts for seamen had been extended to farmers in much of the country; early market data broadcast by the CNR's stations and others had become a regular service; there was live radio drama in most Canadian cities. And all kinds of music, from Guy Lombardo, Percy Faith and Mark Kenny, to the Hart House String Quartet and

Every day was New Year's for Canada's Guy Lombardo and his 'sweetest music this side of heaven.' (CBC Archives)

the Toronto Mendelssohn Choir, were being broadcast in programme schedules that were still 70 per cent music.

The Great Depression made radio irresistible, but it was World War II that made it indispensable. That first "citizens' war" made even North Americans full participants in the appalling events of Europe and Asia. Churchill's speeches, Vera Lynn's songs, Big Ben tolling the introduction of the BBC news, Matthew Halton bringing us the sounds and terrors of the London blitz — each drew us together in a communion of shared experience and common goals.

World War II also marked one of the many periods in broadcast history in which Canadians had a technical lead, later surrendered to our more confident and entrepreneurial American cousins. American correspondents covering the war had no recording facilities; when listeners heard Edward R. Murrow broadcasting sounds of the Luftwaffe over London, the Luftwaffe was there at that moment. But CBC crews, outfitted with broadcast vans that included equipment to make recorded discs, could collect sound from a variety of sources, blend it together with scripted commentary and analysis, and provide much more richly constructed sound documentaries. The CBC reporters could also gather sound material from remote or dangerous battlefront areas where their American competitors could never arrange or obtain live broadcast lines.

A similar situation existed in the mid-sixties, when the level of videotape editing expertise in Canada was a full technical generation ahead of the best facilities available in New York or Hollywood. While we were making sophisticated, electronic edits on videotape, the major American networks were still editing videotapes by cutting them with scissors and fastening the amputated ends together. One result of that technical lag was that Harry Belafonte, never a slow man to recognize talent, was to insist that all of his TV specials be produced out of Toronto's CBC television studios, and directed by a Canadian, Paddy Samson, whose creative gifts were matched by a thorough understanding of the new technology.

In World War II the CBC's capacity to record sound effects led some Canadian reporters to be somewhat cavalier about the events around them. As James M. Minifie, a journalistic veteran of the Spanish Civil War once told me:

"Once, during the Blitz in 1941, Edward Murrow and some of the other correspondents invited me up onto the roof of our London hotel to watch a raid and then down to the Savoy's bar for a drink. But because of the time difference I had to be up in the middle of the night to read a broadcast to Canada, and we already had sound effects of a good raid recorded, so I decided to sleep for a few hours. While I was sleeping, a block-buster landed somewhere nearby and blew in my hotel room windows, and a shard of glass took out my eye as I lay in bed. I've never turned a drink down since!"

What the war also did was create an insatiable appetite in listeners for news broadcasts. And that was a problem because, up to 1939, Canadian radio station journalists could all easily have been fitted into the smallest studio in the country without anyone suffering physical distress or personal indignity. The Canadian anxiety for news from the war fronts was exacerbated by the fact that this country entered the war two years and three months before the United States. Insulated by its neutrality and shielded by the "fortress America" philosophy of the day, the United States was much less concerned about events in Austria, Poland, Czech-

James M. (Don) Mini-fie (left) beside a burned-out tank in the Italian campaign, 1945. (Public Archives of Canada)

oslovakia, Belgium, Holland and China than was Canada. So Canadian listeners could not turn to U.S. stations for coverage of the war.

Broadly speaking, Canadian radio in the pre-war years regarded news as something to be read, not gathered. By the early thirties the Canadian Radio Broadcasting Commission was employing Charles Jennings as Canada's first radio network newscaster. His successor, Lorne Greene, became known during the war as "the voice of doom" for his portentous, basso readings. From 1933 on,

Charles Jennings mimics the stereotypical announcer of the forties, hand over ear to increase the resonance of his voice. (Private collection: Sarah Jennings)

Canadian Press had agreed to provide the CRBC with a daily, 1,200-word news bulletin to be read at 10:45 p.m. nightly on the new network. But the CRBC, like the CBC that was to follow it, took some BBC style to its bosom while missing the best of what was happening across the Atlantic. In the early years of the BBC, announcers were required to wear tuxedos while reading radio news to keep them constantly in mind of the need for dignity and probity in their delivery. Similarly, the CRBC and the CBC were quick to concentrate on the *tone* of newscasts.

But the BBC had moved far beyond mere image, as had broadcast organizations in France, Belgium, Switzerland and Germany, where by 1938 radio reporters were getting equal access to public figures

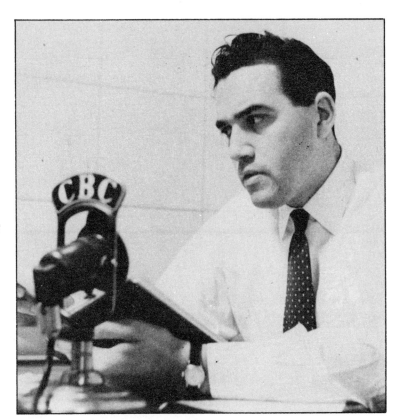

'The voice of doom' at work in a CBC radio studio: Lorne Greene in the late forties. (CBC Archives)

with newspapermen, and gathering, writing and editing their own material. A few private radio stations, most notably CFCN Calgary, developed networks of regional correspondents and gathered their own news from any source available, including telegraph and short-wave radio. But most were content to carry the CP bulletins fed them by the CBC. A few stations owned by newspapers were permitted to carry stories from their owner's newspaper, so long as they weren't broadcast until 30 minutes after the papers hit the streets. Even then some "scoops" were prohibited territory for these stations.

Canadian Press, the news-gathering organization established and owned by Canada's daily newspapers, imposed strict controls to protect its

BBC wasn't the only radio service requiring its announcers to dress as they were meant to sound. This photo is of R. H. Roberts, a CNR announcer in the twenties, in his working clothes. (Canadian National Railways Archives)

print-oriented owners. Newscasts could not be sponsored, as the newspapers were terrified of broadcast competition for advertising dollars. CP also wanted guarantees that only CP bulletins would be broadcast, to the total exclusion of news gathered by any other agency.

There was, too, the continuing concern that state radio would fail to give the public what it wanted. It might, after all, in the words of an *Ottawa Journal* editorial, "get into the control of the visionaries and partisans and uplifters," all noxious types.

By 1939 dissatisfaction with the glacially paced development of broadcast news in Canada led to a new agreement with Canadian Press. CP now agreed to provide its entire news service to the CBC, together with national, regional and local bulletins. The CBC, in return, was to use its "good offices" to persuade private affiliated stations and others to use the CP services, and to make the stories available at cost to stations owned by CP member newspapers.

1939 also brought the awakening of Canadian radio to its capacity to do the job for itself. In 1938, touring Europe for the CBC, Ernie Bushnell had been appalled by the discovery that, "in none of the countries that I have visited have the press or the daily newspapers the control of broadcasting news as is the case in Canada." However, Bushnell had also seen BBC reporters recording a statement from Neville Chamberlain on his return from Munich, while Canadian radio simply provided an announcer to read a transcript of the Chamberlain statement from a newspaper story by Canadian Press. But still it took the royal visit of King George VI and Queen Elizabeth to bring on the stimulus for change.

Canada in 1939 was intensely monarchist, and no one in the country more so than Prime Minister Mackenzie King. The CBC was determined to provide radio coverage as never before, and King's government was of no mind to deny the corporation the resources that it might require. In 1936 the CBC had a total staff of 132, including 19 announcers, 10 producers and 11 clerks. But in May of 1939 the CBC found 100 people just to staff the royal tour, including 13 announcers who were given special courses in pronunciation and protocol at Government House in Ottawa. In six weeks the tour crew travelled 7,000 miles and made 91 broadcasts, while school children from Victoria to Halifax left pennies on the rail lines so they would have personal souvenirs of the royal progression.

CBC *broadcasts of the 1939 royal tour required a triple play: from the announcer, wearing a radio transmitter back-pack (constantly adjusted by his engineer), to the receiver in the mobile van; and thence to the nearest* CBC *studios and transmitter. This trailer, being tested in the Rockies, was the* CBC's *first mobile radio van.* (CBC *Archives*)

Meanwhile, just prior to the royal visit, the CBC had been divided into the tragic, separate and separated English and French divisions which have, tons of press releases notwithstanding, endured and hardened with every year. Everyone concerned with French-language broadcasting was

King George VI made a network broadcast from Winnipeg on Empire Day, May 24, 1939. (Public Archives of Canada)

moved to Montreal that summer, while Ernie Bushnell, who was supervisor of programming, was moved to Toronto where he became, in reality, supervisor of English programming only.

When war broke out in the autumn of 1939, the CBC had mobile equipment used in the field during the royal tour, and staff confident they could broadcast events of the day from any location. The supreme test was bearing down with the momentum of a crack panzer division.

On the evening of December 4, 1939, R. T. (Bob) Bowman was phoned at his Toronto home by Ernie

Canadian sailors being interviewed before joining their convoy for the hazardous North Atlantic run. Such interviews were withheld from broadcast until the convoy had arrived safely in Britain. (CBC Archives)

Bushnell, who asked him to find out how quickly a CBC recording van from the royal tour could be gotten to Halifax and, by the way, whether Bowman, himself, could catch the next train from Toronto's Union Station to Halifax. The train was leaving less than an hour later, and Bowman, a veteran of the royal visit, was broke. No problem; Bushnell borrowed $25 from his wife and met Bowman at the station. All of this without explanation.

But arrival at Halifax answered all questions. A British battleship rode at anchor in the centre of the harbour, and five huge liners — *The Empress of Britain, The Empress of Australia, The Monarch of Bermuda, The Duchess of Bedford* and *The Aquitania* — were moored at the docks, embarking the Canadian First Division. Meantime, a radio engineer, Art Holmes, was "drafted" to go along, and soon joined Bowman for the sailing aboard *The Aquitania*. Holmes arrived just in time for the sailing, and on their arrival in Britain the two broadcast the first actuality sounds of troops in transit over telephone beam to Canada. Holmes spent large parts of the next two years in his recording van in Hyde Park, making sound discs of the German blitz.

Radio At War: 1940-1945

When Bowman and Holmes arrived in London (where they were soon to be joined by Bushnell, seconded to the BBC to advise on wartime propaganda broadcasts to North America), the CBC still had no news service. Two more commentators were sent to England, one French-speaking, and additional translators were hired in Montreal to enable the corporation to rebroadcast BBC bulletins for Francophones. The CBC also arranged to carry BBC news bulletins daily. But while it arranged for the employment of RCMP guards to protect against sabotage of CBC studios and transmitters in locations 4,000 miles from the war, the CBC failed to hire any newsmen until the end of 1940. The annual report for the period ending March 31, 1940 devotes more attention to the initiation of the "Just Mary" series for children, the continuing success of "The Happy Gang" and the development of farm broadcasts than to the organization of a news department. The news organization was, in fact, nothing more than a series of expanded arrangements to transmit CP and BBC data via CBC announcers and transmitters.

Perhaps because it had been partly paralyzed by the trauma of "Uncle Sage," the CBC retained a foot-dragging attitude towards news coverage for decades. It wasn't until 1959 that it made a concerted effort to obtain entry to the Ottawa press gallery. It was safer until then to use CP and add voice commentaries from newspapermen who, as

freelance contributors, absolved the CBC of corporate guilt for any politically embarrassing things
they might say. Thanks also to the obstruction of
gallery members, who didn't wish to lose that
lucrative CBC income, CBC's first Ottawa correspondent, Tom Earle, covered the House of Commons
from the diplomatic gallery for two years until his
print colleagues relented, admitting both Earle
and private broadcaster Sam Ross in December,
1961. By then TV was a muscular infant prodigy
and also had to be admitted to gallery membership.

It was late in 1940 before CBC radio felt itself

*Tom Earle on location.
(CBC Archives)*

impelled to actually edit news itself. Dan McArthur was appointed head of the CBC national news service, and plans were laid for regional news bureaus in Vancouver, Halifax, Winnipeg, Toronto and Montreal. In early December, according to one CBC history, all senior editors (five in number, presumably) assembled in Toronto, where they were given a full "course of instruction" lasting for one week. They then had "a two-week period of practice" before the CBC national news service began a regular schedule of broadcasts on January 1, 1941. How much practice was exercised between the Christmas and New Year's holiday is mercifully shrouded in historic confusion. But lest you doubt what can be accomplished in a one-week training course, here's a description of events from the CBC annual report of March 31, 1941:

"An effort was made to establish an acceptable style for the CBC news bulletins and all those present had much practice in writing copy in the idiom and rhythm of ordinary speech, intended for the ear rather than for the eye. At the same time, problems of policy, organization and personnel were thoroughly discussed and clarified."

Not bad for a five-day course. Mind you, the staff was selected on the grounds that "dependability was naturally a major consideration." Not that reporting skill was essential, nor even desirable. These were "editors," people entrusted with translating wire copy into broadcast English (or French, in Montreal, which had twinned staffs to function in both languages). The bureaucrats who wrote the annual report put it somewhat more persuasively:

"In order that CBC bulletins should be more than mere re-writes of news dispatches, a library of up-to-date reference books was established at each bureau, together with a file of clippings on domestic and foreign affairs, personalities, etc., which would provide background material for quick and authoritative reference."

So there. But 40 years later neither CBC nor any other broadcast organization in Canada has developed the confidence in its own staff, for example, to emulate the Time-Life empire which keeps as its most valuable reference data lengthy, massively detailed, confidential memos filed by every reporter during and after every major assignment. Most Canadian broadcast executives remain intellectually hobbled by the continuing gut conviction, contrary to their every public pronouncement, that it is likely more reliable if it's been in print.

During the war years both Canadian Press and British United Press continued to supply CBC, and through CBC most private Canadian stations, with free wire service. It was a perfect marriage between fiscal probity and moral cowardice. Nor were the private radio stations much displeased by the arrangement. They were, for openers, terrified of running afoul of wartime censorship regulation, a pitfall totally obviated by their use of pre-digested CBC and CP copy. Moreover, the competitor (CBC) was also, as the broadcast regulator, the referee in its own game, capable, at least theoretically, of lifting the licence of non-complying private stations.

Pronunciation was a problem for all broadcasters during the war. Again quoting from the CBC annual report of 1941:

"The spreading of the war to various parts of the world and the subsequent appearance in the news of strange place names and personal names have created a difficult problem for announcers. The policy consistently followed by the CBC has been to consult the best available printed and personal authorities, and *to pronounce foreign names with such an approximation to the correct pronunciation as will leave the announcer free from the charge either of conscious superiority or careless ignorance. It is always to be borne in mind that a foreign name must not be so pronounced as to be unrecognizable to the ordinary listener."* (author's emphasis)

This was a pragmatic balance in CBC terms between accuracy and the limited capacities of the ordinary, Chicago-survey listener.

In addition, the CBC had a set of ten policy directives with regard to the preparation and presentation of all news broadcasts. A few of those were:

a) Only news from Canadian Press, British United Press or CBC news staff should be used. No one outside the CBC "may be given payment for news, direct or indirect."

b) "Crime stories, where they have sufficient general interest to be used at all, should be handled with discretion. Remember that they go into the home, and may be heard at unsuitable times."

c) "News should be handled so as not to create alarm."

d) "Domestic political news must be treated with absolute impartiality. In controversial stories, both sides of the issue must be given equal emphasis."

e) "No libelous or scandalous news should be permitted ... nor should voice inflection be allowed in any way to colour the news."

f) "No suicide stories — unless about prominent figures; and even these should be very carefully handled."

g) "The canons of good taste should apply, particularly in referring to physical handicaps or deformities."

h) "No stories about lotteries, gambling odds, or any reference to any sports news that would cause people to gamble on the outcome."

However, 40 years later CBC personnel were regularly and cheerfully wagering on air about the outcome of major sports events, even interviewing professional gamblers on the odds being offered. CBC newscasts were announcing the results of *government* lotteries. And in 1979 the corporation, anxious to avoid losing the jocks in its audience, promulgated a regulation that *every* radio newscast had to include at least two sports items — a fiat that resulted in bemused listeners frequently hearing the results of the Patagonian tree-frog jumping contest or of a hernia study among girls' high-school basketball teams. These items occurred on evenings when CP wires failed to produce items of relevance, or when news editors, working alone, were simply unable to discriminate between what mattered and what didn't in a field foreign to them. The whole, silly exercise was a classic example of what happens when arbitrary, quantitative, engineering or administrative requirements are imposed on what's essentially a creative process (or what happens when former sportscasters become programme czars).

Never mind. In 1941 Canada had 2,415,285 families, give or take a few, and there were 1,558,060 radio receiving sets in our homes. There were beginning to be a few in our cars, too, but these were still chiefly the preserve of the wealthy. To service those homes and radios the CBC news service, within a year of its beginning, had moved to occupy one broadcast hour in every five on the radio network. Twenty-five private station affiliates carried all of those newscasts, and they were offered free to every other station in the country. Neither had CBC news staff been persuaded to wear tuxedos, although contemporary pictures indicate an almost universal addiction to white shirts and vests.

Rules are made to be broken, of course, and the CBC wasn't long in utterly dismembering any notion that in matters of domestic political news, when controversial, "both sides of the issue must be given equal emphasis." An opportunity to test that pious policy was quick to arrive, in the early spring of 1942, in the form of a campaign on the question of army conscription. Prime Minister Mackenzie King, eager to avoid exacerbating relations with Quebec, where much of the population was less than lukewarm in support of "England's War," had promised at the beginning of World War II there would be no conscription in Canada. By late 1941 King was less sure that had been a good policy. To avoid any appearance of breaking his promise, he proposed an April, 1942 plebiscite to test the will of the Canadian people, still with a solemn undertaking there was no early conscription on the horizon.

Having announced the plebiscite in the January Throne Speech, King himself made two speeches in support of it on CBC. The second, just three days before the national vote, implied a clear threat that he would resign if the country turned down the principle of conscription. Said King: "If I did not believe that, as head of the Government, I continued to enjoy the confidence of the people, who time and again have returned me to office, I would not wish to remain in office an hour longer."

King's colleagues, too, took to the airwaves to rally support for the "yes" vote. But the CBC, deliberately breaking its own equal-time policy, refused to permit any foe of conscription so much as a moment of air time. The doctrine of "equal emphasis" was never in the running against a comment in the 1941 annual report that, "the principal tasks of the Corporation during this period ... were ... to link the war effort more closely to the life of the individual Canadian in order to inspire his confidence, to strengthen his daily effort, and to stimulate his growing desire to play the fullest possible part in his country's struggle."

Even the programme schedule was at the service of those imperatives. Soon the corporation was to move its nightly national news bulletin back from 11 p.m. eastern time to 10 p.m., so that war workers could go to bed earlier and thus be rested for their efforts the following day.

The war brought on another programme change: since many radio performers were overseas in the army, there was a slight moderation of the stringent regulations prohibiting the use of recorded material. In 1941 the CBC was still arbiter and regulator of all Canadian broadcasting, a role it shed only in 1958, when an independent regulatory body was established by John Diefenbaker and his new government colleagues. At that time many of the new Conservative ministers were suspicious of links between the CBC and the Liberals they had replaced. Most of them were also, and rather accurately, persuaded that under the CBC and during the Liberal government, new and profitable broadcast licences had been granted in Canada only to Liberal applicants. In any event, in 1941, acting as regulator, the CBC generously allowed that it would permit private radio stations to include "one half-hour of recorded or transcribed programmes" between 7:30 p.m. and 11 p.m., "provided that their annual expenditure on live talent satisfies the Corporation's requirements." Some other exceptions were to be permitted at the corporation's pleasure "for stations of low power and in communities where talent is scarce."

The CBC's own view of "talent" was as patronizing as ever. Said a wartime annual report, "During the last year Canadian plays of a very even quality have been produced; they demonstrate that some Canadian authors and playwrights now have a competent knowledge of this new medium."

By the war years drama was mostly the preserve of the CBC, as were major musical programmes. Before formation of the CRBC, the private stations, largely through the CNR network, had combined their meagre resources to provide "chain" or "network" broadcasts to which each made a contribution. But with the CBC in exclusive possession of the right to network broadcasting in Canada, the chances of major programme investments by individual private stations were rapidly diminishing. They were not to revive until the seventies, when microwave transmission and easy sound tape dubbing services made it practical and economic to exchange programme material without formal network links. But, with the exception of some play-by-play sports events, network broadcasting finished for private Canadian stations in 1936.

In the late forties and fifties some stations tried to emulate a form of network broadcasting by exchanging recordings by mail, first on acetate discs, later on sound tape. Many a radio announcer in the mid-fifties, this one included, had to script and then imitate a sports commentator from a distant city whenever the Royal Canadian Mails failed to deliver a taped commentary already scheduled and promoted for broadcast as part of a coast-to-coast round-up of opinion; all of that carefully scripted and edited to sound like a live network broadcast.

Many private stations soldiered on in the effort to produce original dramas, but the realities eventually killed most such enterprises. Some survived

Making a 16-inch acetate recording. (CBC Archives)

CBC-developed equipment used to check the quality of acetate recordings. (CBC Archives)

well into the fifties when a number of stations
(CFAC Calgary is an excellent example) presented
weekly dramatized news magazines, with each
actor playing characters ranging from Charles de
Gaulle to a Brazilian customs official. Usually on
such programmes the producer was also the director and script writer; the sound engineer also had
to create all the sound effects; and these broadcasts were genuinely live with all the attendant
hazards.

In response to a growing clamour for a second
radio network, in 1943 the CBC created one of its
own, chiefly as a vehicle for American programmes
which it then sold to sponsors for additional revenue. The new network, called the Dominion Network, actually consisted of just one CBC station in
Toronto, together with 34 private, affiliated stations,
when it went on the air on January 1, 1944. The
already existing Trans-Canada Network comprised
six CBC stations and 28 private affiliates. It continued to carry the cultural programmes. At this time
the CBC also had three stations in Quebec, together
with 10 private affiliates which carried CBC French-
language broadcasts.

The Dominion Network, later to be succeeded by
the CBC's fm network — which has been on and off
the air in various years depending on the state of
the CBC budget at any given time — survived until
1962, but its demise was clear by the mid-fifties,
when evening audiences began turning from radio
to television. By that time the CBC was getting more
evening commercial revenue from acquired American TV shows than from American radio, so the
extra radio chain was doomed.

The dichotomy between expressions of confidence in Canadian production ("Canadian plays of
very even quality") and the lust for British and
American programmes which draw a bigger audi-

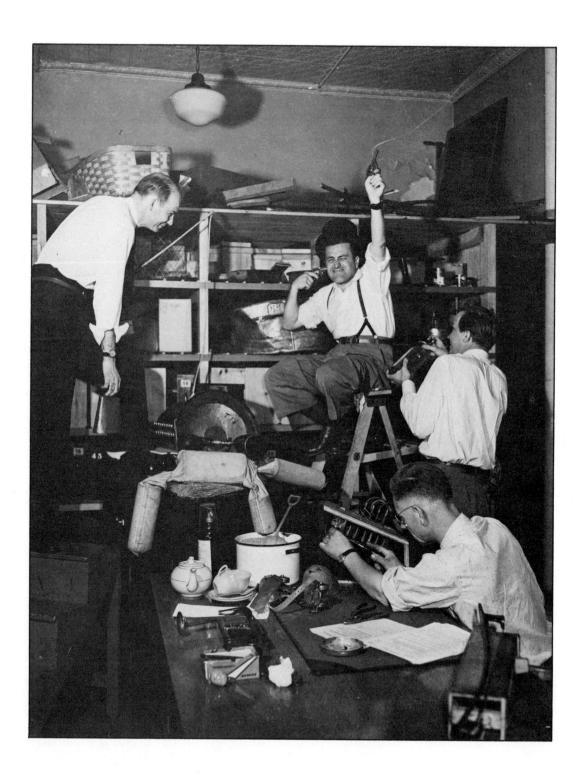

◁CBC *sound effects engineers at play. (Ontario Archives: Gilbert W. Milne Collection)*

The all-purpose sound effects door, this one photographed at CKAC *Montreal in 1931. (Public Archives of Canada)*

ence and, therefore, a bigger harvest of commercial dollars has been a constant in Canadian broadcasting. The same annual report of the CBC which paid that left-handed compliment to creative Canadians proudly recited a catalogue of broadcast plays featuring such actors as Paul Muni, Herbert Marshall, Walter Huston, Alfred Lunt, Madeleine Carroll, Lynne Fontanne, Raymond Massey (loaned back to Canada by Hollywood), Edmund Gwynn, Anna Neagle and Sir Cedric and Lady Hardwicke. Even New York's mayor, Fiorello LaGuardia, helped out.

Before the United States entered the war in December, 1941, American writers and performers sympathetic to the Allied cause were wooed to Canada to inspire us to buy War Savings Stamps and to extend ourselves in war industry. One such performer, the trenchant Dorothy Thompson, gave a radio talk of such persuasive power that the CBC received 60,000 requests for printed copies of her remarks. That number and its evidence of listener loyalty and interest are stunning; so much mail in the fourth decade of television would put any TV producer on the continent into spasms of lethal delight. To put that mail response in context: in 1966, during the last weeks of the CBC programme "This Hour Has Seven Days," the programme got as many as 3,000 to 4,000 letters and cards from viewers each week. No one in CBC could conceive of so much viewer mail or loyalty. But in that earlier, more innocent age, Miss Thompson had garnered 15 times as much mail from a single, scripted talk on radio.

Part of the key to listener attention lay in the emphasis, continued through the forties, on community service by radio. For example, the Northern Messenger, initiated in 1933, was still a staple of CBC Friday broadcasting through the war. Listeners

The Northern Messenger in action; Christmas carols on the air. Left to right: Bob Willson, Rene Dussault, Harry Randall (the producer), Lorne Wallace, Norm Micklewright and George Rich. (CBC Archives)

could hear that "Sally arrived at the hospital in Yellowknife ok, and she has a fine baby boy." They were given personal messages of arrivals and departures, of medical services, aerial deliveries of food and other supplies, weather forecasts and the like. And in a new but similar service, British children "orphaned" to the Dominion for the period of the blitz were able to talk from CBC studios in Canada with their parents in BBC studios in London as part of a weekly broadcast.

Overseas, meanwhile, the small contingent of CBC announcers and technicians gathered and recorded messages for home from Canadian servicemen, who penned them in the British Isles during the long haul between the fall of Dunkirk and the Dieppe raid and the subsequent invasions of Sicily and Italy. When our troops finally went to

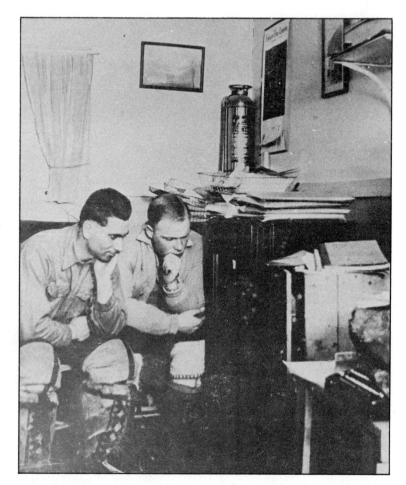

The other end of the tube; listeners to the Northern Messenger in a remote arctic settlement. (CBC Archives)

the continent, CBC's vans went along (one had been armoured to protect the precious recording equipment inside), and the messages continued to be relayed, from foxholes and hospital wards alike, to relatives and friends at home. During 1941, the CBC recording van in London collected "several holes made by bomb splinters and shrapnel," but no "serious damage" beyond "one or two close calls."

The BBC did its bit by rebroadcasting NHL hockey games, recorded and edited in Canada, on the Sunday morning following the Saturday night

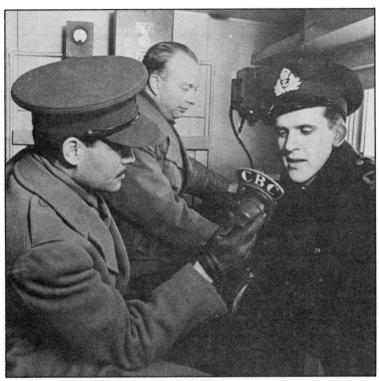

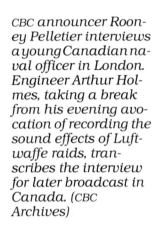

CBC announcer Rooney Pelletier interviews a young Canadian naval officer in London. Engineer Arthur Holmes, taking a break from his evening avocation of recording the sound effects of Luftwaffe raids, transcribes the interview for later broadcast in Canada. (CBC Archives)

games here, so that our troops could hear the play-by-play coverage. This prompted one Nazi propaganda broadcaster, a lady who seemed to like Foster Hewitt, to suggest Canadians should "forget the war and go home to your hockey."

Through the war years radio became a habit and an obsession. Governmental recognition of its vast impact as a tool of war policy loosened purse strings (well, a little). Those who grew up in the radio of the forties knew themselves to be in the most exciting and secure growth industry in our society. And it was to stay that way for almost 15 years after the war ended. But the usurper of radio's throne was waiting impatiently in the wings, needing only the war's end to free the creative and industrial capacity which would lend it the polish and sophistication required of those on centre

*Peter Stursberg inter-
viewing an* RAF *squad-
ron leader, Jack Char-
les, in Kent, in early
1943. (Public Archives
of Canada)* ▷

◁CBC mobile unit number 4 in Italy, 1943. From left to right: Mathew Halton, Captain John Howard, Marcel Ouimet, A. J. MacDonald, P. F. Johnson, Peter Stursberg. (Public Archives of Canada)

CBC correspondent Marcel Ouimet at the Italian front, 1943. (Public Archives of Canada)

stage. Television pictures had first been shown in England in 1926 by John Logie Baird. After their public debut in Canada, nothing would ever be quite the same.

TELEVISION

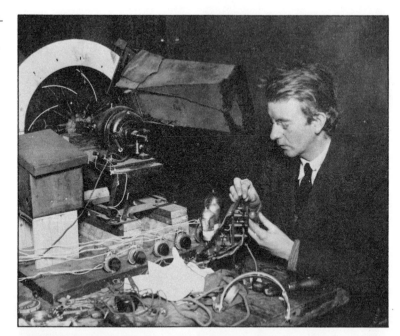

March, 1925: John Logie Baird adjusting his first crude picture transmitter. (BBC Hulton Picture Library)

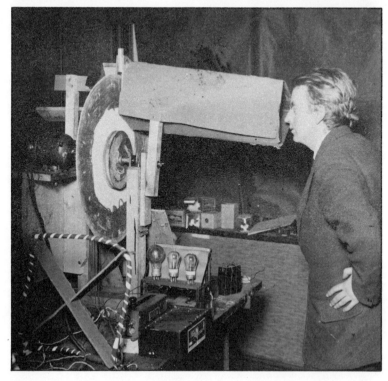

Baird looking at the picture received from his 'flying disc' television transmitter. (BBC Hulton Picture Library)

The Birth of the Boob-Tube: 1925-1952

The origins of television lie in the nineteenth century, in the fertile minds of a British telegrapher and a German inventor, although neither had any notion of the potential inherent in their studies. In 1873 the Brit, a gentleman named May (even his first name seems lost in the mist of history; the Encyclopaedia Britannica refers to him simply as L. May) discovered that light could be changed into electrical impulses. Eleven years later the German, a man now known only as P. Nipkow, filed a patent for a system of analyzing and synthesizing images so that they could be transmitted over a single "channel" electrically.

It took a Scot, John Logie Baird, to meld the two discoveries, and in 1924, 40 years after Nipkow's first patent, to transmit the image of the outline of an object. By 1925 Baird was "televising" a "recognizable human face," and in 1926 he was ready for a full demonstration of the first real TV picture before the Royal Academy in London. By 1928 Baird, like Fessenden before him, was working with ships; that year Baird sent a TV picture to the good ship *Berengaria* in mid-Atlantic. Baird was hired by the German post office to develop a television system for them, and his invention was used both by Germany and England in 1936, in the initial stages of each country's TV transmission. Although his "first generation" equipment was soon abandoned in both countries, Baird contin-

John Baird in 1938, demonstrating the latest in modern television receivers. (BBC Hulton Picture Library)

ued to work in TV development. In 1937 he demonstrated a colour television transmitter, and in 1946 he was reported to have developed a stereoscopic TV picture (3-D we'd call it now) just before his death.

The Baird system was fundamentally mechanical rather than electronic. It used a large, rotating metal disc which contained from 60 to 120 small, square holes arranged in a circular, concentric line starting at the edge of the plate. Rotating 20 times per second, the disc scanned one line of the picture or image through each hole. The lines, fed through the holes in the disc to a photo-electric cell, were translated into electrical impulses which were fed to a second system in the receiver. There, a second disc, rotating in synchronization with the first, reversed the process, and turned the electrical impulses back into light lines which, assembled on a TV screen, produced pictures. As the human eye and optic nerve have a tenth-of-a-second "memory," or time lag, images which occur at a frequency greater than 1/10 of a second seem to flow together as we watch them. The 20 pictures per second produced by Baird was enough to fool the optic nerve and its components, and produce "moving pictures" for television. Even on Baird's tiny picture screen, less than five inches in diameter, the 120-line picture was more blur than photo; it lacked resolution and sharp definition. But it impressed.

Sir John Aird visited Baird in London in 1932, and posed for a televised portrait. He told the radio committee in Ottawa on his return, "I was a subject of television at the Baird Works in London and was very impressed... television is not perfected yet... but it is coming, gentlemen, and we should be prepared... It is not impossible that television will someday... become of importance."

That same year, 1932, a British engineer named Douglas West, who had worked with Baird in England, formed Canadian Television Limited in Montreal. By offering shares in his new company both to Baird and to C. F. Jenkins in the United States (whose inventions closely paralleled Baird's), West was able to obtain Canadian rights to their developments. A young McGill engineering student, Alphonse Ouimet, was just about to graduate that year. Hearing of the new company through his uncle, who had rented office and laboratory space to West, he applied for a job as the company's first research engineer. West gave the young graduate two of Baird's scanning discs, a handful of photo-electric cells, "a rather temperamental amplifier" (Ouimet's words); and told the youth to design and build a transmitter, synchronizing motor and receiver, so television could be demonstrated to Canadians. West also provided a machinist, a metal lathe, a drill press, a couple of work benches, and a division of labour: Alphonse Ouimet was to build a television set while West worked the Montreal financial community to raise the necessary money.

The 60-line picture then being developed, compared with 525 lines on today's TV, provided at best what Ouimet called "a very coarse picture which barely showed enough detail to recognize one's own mother on a full-face close-up." BBC used a papier mâché mannequin for test pictures, but West couldn't afford one. As Ouimet, who eventually became president of CBC, described in a reminiscence:

"We used to take turns before the "flying spot camera," while others made the necessary changes in the equipment. I was in greater demand than the others as a dummy because...on a close-up of my face, if one could make out the grand canyon between my upper, central incisors, we knew we were getting all the definition that could possibly be squeezed out of our equipment. Not only am I one of Canada's first television pioneers, I was certainly its first test pattern."

Canadian Television Limited's Montreal workshop in 1932; Alphonse Ouimet is at the workbench. (Private collection: Alphonse Ouimet)

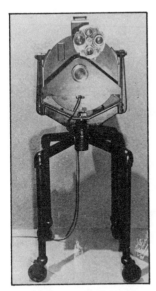

A 1931 TV studio camera; the 'flying disc' developed by Baird was housed inside. (Public Archives of Canada)

In the summer of 1932 the first crude pictures *sans* sound were transmitted over facilities borrowed from station CKAC Montreal. By October, after sporadic transmissions, West had decided that a truly public demonstration was in order, so the company's one and only TV receiver was put on display in the Ogilvie Department Store on St. Catherine Street. A glinch in the circuits kept changing the picture from positive to negative, and it wasn't even black and white. Because the actual picture was created through a neon tube, it was black and red. But it was a picture, and it moved. About 100,000 people lined up for a momentary glimpse of the shimmering technical marvel, and Montreal's four department stores placed orders for 100 receiving sets! But West had to turn to the Marconi Company to manufacture the sets and Marconi wanted a $35,000 deposit. West couldn't raise the money. Canadian Television Limited went belly up. West went into obscurity; Ouimet went to the brand-new Canadian Radio Broadcasting Commission; and television went into mothballs in Canada, not to emerge until 30 years later. In September, 1952, 26 years after BBC began regular TV service, 24 years after France went into television, and six years after the Americans began wholesale television, two CBC-TV stations went, just barely, on the air in Montreal and Toronto.

In the interval, RCA of the United States had invested $50 million to develop an electronic scanning system which provided a sharply defined picture of 525 individual lines, rendering Baird's gritty 60-line picture obsolete. The RCA development had been ready before the war, but priority on wartime arms production delayed manufacture and marketing plans until 1947. A half-dozen experimental TV stations operated in the United States during the war years, but there were fewer

CBC President Alphonse Ouimet with a model of the TV receiver he designed and built in 1932. (CBC Archives)

than 10,000 sets in the entire country. By 1949 the number of home receivers had jumped to a million. In 1951, a full year before CBC broadcast its first TV picture, Americans owned more than 10 million television sets. That same year, 1951, Americans saw their first coast-to-coast microwaved live TV programme.

CBFT Montreal launched its inaugural telecast on September 6, 1952. Two days later Toronto viewers (there were already about 146,000 TV sets in Canada, purchased to view American border stations like those in Buffalo and Detroit) were treated to the CBC's first English-language television programme.

November 30, 1951. In a demonstration of television in the CBC radio building on Dorchester Street in Montreal, the witnesses (and guinea pigs) were, left to right: CBC Board of Governors Chairman A. Davidson Dunton, House of Commons Radio Committee Chairman W. A. Robinson, and Tory MP (later finance minister) Donald Fleming. (Public Archives of Canada)

What they saw first was the station's call letters, CBLT. And they were upside down.

The initial evening's programming on CBLT ran for three hours, from 7:15 until 10:15 p.m. It opened with a preview of the evening's entertainment, then Percy Saltzman gave the weather forecast. By March, 1953 Saltzman had been hired by

The CBC in Toronto took its first TV cameras to the Canadian National Exhibition in August, 1952 to get some practical location experience. (Private collection: Drew Crossan)

Ross MacLean, Canada's first and best public affairs television producer, to act as an interviewer on the new programme, "Tabloid." But MacLean didn't think Percy looked quite right on camera. The breezy weatherman, already known and loved for his tricky, one-handed tosses and catches of his chalk at the end of each forecast, thus became the first Canadian experiment in "TV image." MacLean ordered a pair of horn-rimmed eyeglasses from props. Percy tried them on and MacLean decided the image was perfect, this despite the fact the frames were absolutely innocent of glass. Saltzman went on wearing the glass-less frames in TV appearances over the next 25 years.

The opening festivities on CBLT also included a brief news magazine (run twice, at 7:30 and 10

*September 8, 1952. The TV control room on CBLT's opening
night: Drew Crossan (seated, in black sweater with white
trim) is between his technical producer and script assistant; producer Mavor Moore is talking on the telephone. (CBC
Archives)*

p.m.), a 45-minute variety package, a half hour
with the Leslie Bell Singers (a choir made famous
on CBC radio), and a 30-minute variety programme
supplied by the pioneer TV station in Canada, CBFT
Montreal, which had already been on the air for
two days. CBC Chairman Davidson Dunton spoke
some words of welcome; and appropriately, given

Percy Saltzman, chalk on the fly. (CBC Archives)

Pre-show pep talk by Drew Crossan on September 8, 1952. Among the cast facing him: Don Harron (biting his nails, extreme left), Glenn Gould (in white gloves), John Fisher, Wally Koster, Jan Rubes, Terry Dale, Fran Wright, Dave Price, Ted Reeve, Geoffrey Waddington. Mavor Moore, on the right, examines his opening-night script. (CBC Archives)

The movers and shakers stand beside camera one in CBLT's studio on opening night. They are, left to right: Fergus Mutrie, Dr. J. J. McCann, Davidson Dunton, and Ernie Bushnell, whose Levantine ploys got the station on the air on schedule. (CBC Archives)

that CBC government subsidies were aiming for the $100 million plus mark, so did Dr. J. J. McCann, Canada's minister of national revenue. Never mind that a combination of timidity in the CBC and foot-dragging on Parliament Hill had delayed things for a decade, that the United States had made a coast-to-coast TV microwave telecast a year earlier, or that 30 years had lapsed between Alphonse Ouimet's Montreal demonstration and the appearance of CBLT — none of that mattered. All that was important was that television had arrived. It might, indeed, "someday, become of importance." The great adventure had begun.

Television was around to stay, and for the CBC so was the now permanent gulf between the two solitudes of French and English language and culture. One example: In a biography of Ernie Bushnell, who virtually manhandled CBLT onto the air on schedule by brute force and a breathtaking series of bureaucratic end runs, there is virtually no mention at all of the parallel struggle to get CBFT on the air in Montreal. Even before the inaugural telecasts, the French and English divisions of CBC were beyond reconciliation. In its first years CBC experimented with bilingual telecasts, switching from programmes in one language to the other. After Ernie Bushnell obtained the licence for station CJOH in Ottawa, he tried the same technique. Both failed utterly. Viewers of both cultures telephoned and wrote insults that left phone receptionists and mail clerks in tears.

Curiously the CBC, with its considerable experience of radio and the knowledge that every Canadian home with television certainly possessed at least one radio receiver, never considered telecasts in one language with simulcast radio transmission of a sound track in the other, so that one broadcast service could serve both languages. Such a service would have had all of Canada watching *the same television*. The benefits to English viewers, able to enjoy the extraordinary explosion of French creative talent in the fifties and sixties, would have been incalculable. Moreover, such a two-way simulcast system might have created a mutual understanding, and obviated the sense of isolation and the bunker mentality that inevitably led Quebec from the "Quiet Revolution" of the late fifties and early sixties to the election 20 years later of a government dedicated to taking that province out of Confederation.

Certainly it was the CBC, ubiquitous at major

Canadian events since its formation, which contributed most to the politicization of the leader of that government, Rene Lévesque. Lévesque, the most effective Canadian television performer ever, in both languages, was host in 1958 of the wildly popular "Point de Mire," a virtuoso one-man show of public affairs analysis. When CBC's French-language producers went on strike at the corporation in December, 1958, Lévesque was appalled by the inept and ham-fisted way the public broadcasting agency handled the negotiations. Among other things, the CBC despatched two senior management negotiators to deal with the strikers, both of whom were equally unable to utter a word of French. Prime Minister John Diefenbaker's government was unsympathetic; his labour minister repeatedly refused to help arbitrate the 69-day strike. And organizations of English-speaking producers stayed aloof from the dispute. In Lévesque's words, 20 years later:

"The whole bloody French network became virtually non-existent, and nobody cared. Here Radio-Canada was supposed to be so vital a part of the CBC — it was so important to broadcast in French. But Ottawa didn't give a damn. And the non-Quebec labour unions tried to stab us in the back . . . I learned then that French was really very secondary in the rest of Canada's mind, certainly in Ottawa's."

A 22-year-old failed law student in 1944, Rene Lévesque had broadcast from London for the U.S. Office of War Information as a uniformed correspondent. A decade later he was covering the Korean War for the CBC with conspicuous courage and imagination. But on March 2, 1959 Lévesque was arrested outside the Radio-Canada building in Montreal during a demonstration connected with the producers' strike. And in 1960, after a

War correspondent Rene Lévesque interviews Canadian Private Lawrence Hall in a mortar position behind communist lines north of the Imjin River in Korea on August 14, 1951. (Public Archives of Canada)

brief post-strike return to "Point de Mire," Rene Lévesque was elected to Quebec's National Assembly. He never looked back, just as CBC in such matters never looked ahead.

There was a further irony when, in 1963, Prime Minister Mike Pearson, in an attempt to placate a rising tide of expectation in Quebec, named Davidson Dunton co-chairman of a federal commission to study biculturalism and bilingualism. Dunton, one of Canada's most urbane, civilized and engaging sons, had been easily the most brilliant man ever appointed to head the CBC, a job from which he'd retired in 1958. But he had been the boss for

Rene Lévesque balances his spring-wound, battery-operated tape recorder on his head as he fords a Korean river in 1951. (Public Archives of Canada)

seven years in 1952, when television began, and under him the corporation had already lost its best opportunity to play the unifying role which had, from the beginning, been seen as its main task.

Gaucheries and Glamour: TV in the Fifties

While the Ottawa mandarins struggled with the need to begin a television system for Canada, radio was going from strength to strength. Andrew Allan had begun production of his matchless "Drama Stage" series in 1944 with "Stage '44." It became a training ground for a cadre of actors without whom, as Tyrone Guthrie later said, the development of the Stratford Festival would have been impossible. Johnny Wayne and Frank Schuster came home from the war in 1945 and were soon writing and starring in the "Johnny Home Show," followed in 1946 by the first "Wayne and Schuster Show." Harry Boyle, who'd begun his career as a

Kate Aitken (right), the doyenne of CBC radio, at a 'tasting contest' in Toronto in 1944. (Ontario Archives: Gilbert W. Milne Collection)

The blonde is a French teacher, and Johnny Wayne and Frank Schuster do a little apple polishing in a bilingual comedy sketch in October, 1953. (Public Archives of Canada)

Canada's best-known comedy team in a familiar role in the sixties. (CBC Archives)

In 1960 Andrew Allan launched the experimental TV drama series "Q for Quest" with the controversial play "Burlap Bags," directed by Daryl Duke and written by Len Peterson. (CBC Archives)

Never one to let grass grow under his lip, Harry Boyle clowns with a friendly clarinet. (CBC Archives)

May, 1948: a CBC radio production of Gilbert and Sullivan's "HMS Pinafore." Radio offered more freedom than television: musicians could play in their shirt sleeves, and singers awaiting their next chorus could catch up on their knitting. (Ontario Archives: Gilbert W. Milne Collection)

farm commentator in a rural Ontario station (CKNX Wingham) had come aboard and was running the Trans-Canada Network for CBC. Boyle, later to serve as chairman of the Canadian Radio-Television Commission, did more than any other broadcaster to encourage and develop young public affairs writers and broadcasters, myself included, back in the mid-fifties. Between them, Andrew Allan and Harry Boyle discovered and created a generation of skilled writers and performers. The best credentials both had lay in their own considerable creative gifts. Boyle was then, and after his retirement

Everybody wants to be somebody else: in this forties gag-shot, actors impersonate musicians. John Drainie is attacking the violin on the far left, as is Lorne Greene beside him. Bernie Braden is trying to master the horn while Alfie Scopp wields the cello. That's Mavor Moore playing the cardboard-box-with-cords; Alice Hill, behind him, is seated in front of Don Harron, who is playing the trombone by scalp rather than by ear. Lloyd Bochner is in the extreme rear, left. (Private collection: Bronwyn Drainie)

from the CRTC, a prolific freelance writer, and both men were gifted essayists.

Radio's momentum kept those golden days alive until the mid-to-late fifties. But before that time, television's high impact, high pay and glamour were seducing actors and writers along with audiences. A few gifted and dedicated folk stayed doggedly with the senior service. Robert Weaver, for example, nourished and sustained scores of Canadian writers when, through the fifties and sixties, they were an endangered species. He deserves a

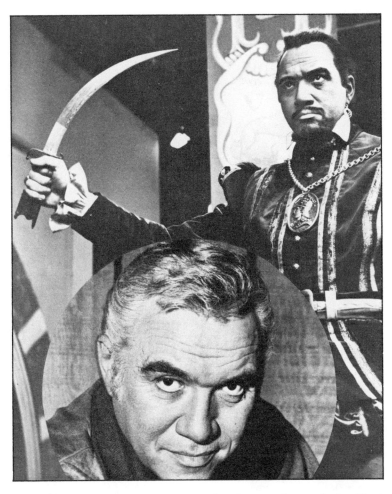

*Lorne Greene as
Othello and, in the in-
sert, as Pa Cartwright.
(CBC Archives)*

medal and retroactive pay for hazardous duty. But
Weaver was an exception.

As early as 1953 Lorne Greene, later seen as Pa
Cartwright on TV sets from Tokyo to Berlin, moved
from his niche as the voice of doom to play the
Prince of the Moors in a CBC television adaptation
of "Othello." Mind you, lest viewers be confused by
the blackface make-up (shades of the CNR min-
strels of 30 years earlier), the CBC issued press
release photos of Greene in his Othello make-up
and costume with a real-life portrait of himself, as
himself, cunningly superimposed over Othello's
tummy.

In "Julius Caesar"
Lorne Greene brooded
darkly with a youth-
ful William Shatner,
who was still years
away from trading
his lute for the com-
mand deck of the star-
ship Enterprise. (CBC
Archives)

There were still dark suspicions of television.
Said a Toronto school trustee in 1952, "It gives the
children bad eyes, makes them unable to sleep and
unable to study." Said Mavor Moore, then chief
producer for CBC English TV, "We hope to be on the
air for two hours nightly to begin with ... We don't
want to put on anything unless and until we think
it's ready and good enough for you to see." Thirty
years later Moore was head of the Canada Council.

Since many radio producers and stars preferred
to stay where they were, still buoyed by the eupho-
ria of the postwar boom, TV producers like Ross
MacLean built new stars. Percy Saltzman, Toby

© 1976. Reprinted with permission of the *Toronto Star* Syndicate

"O.K. Kiddies, Bedtime."

Parents were still concerned about the effects of TV on their children in the mid-seventies. In 1978 former Secretary of State Judy LaMarsh chaired an Ontario Royal Commission on the impact of violence on television. (Duncan MacPherson in the Toronto Star)

Robbins, Pierre Berton, Charles Templeton, Elaine Grande and Joyce Davidson soon became as familiar to Canadian TV viewers as Fibber McGee and Jack Benny. Juliette joined band leader Billy O'Connor and made a smooth transition to TV. Robert Goulet divided his hours between serenading girlfriends in a walk-up flat in a seedy section of downtown

*Billy O'Connor (at pi-
ano) doing the Coca-
Cola Show with sing-
er Sylvia Murphy. (Pri-
vate collection: Sylvia
Murphy)*

Ross MacLean at work — proving that genius was 99 per cent perspiration and concentration. (CBC Archives)

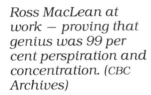

◁ *Even the little fingers were rehearsed and posed as Robert Goulet and Joyce Sullivan accepted a toast and took a bow on live fifties television. (CBC Archives)*

Toronto, and wowing audiences from a CBC-TV studio before moving to the big time in New York (where he scored his greatest publicity coup by forgetting, in a night club performance, the words to "The Star Spangled Banner").

Joyce Davidson sought the greener pastures, too, after her contract was not renewed. That latter act subsequent to a public outcry after the lovely Miss Davidson, on the eve of the royal tour in 1959, told viewers that "I, like most Canadians, am rather indifferent to the Queen's visit." Miss Davidson's stardom on Ross MacLean's "Tabloid" programme notwithstanding, Ernie Bushnell had her suspended. After her marriage in New York to

Jack Kane (left) led the orchestra on "The Musicmakers" and gave Canadian viewers the best big band music since the forties. Sylvia Murphy is beside him, along with Joyce Davidson and Bill Walker. (Private collection: Sylvia Murphy)

TV film production maestro David Susskind, the still-gorgeous Miss Davidson returned to Canada as a commuter in the late seventies, hosting an interview series on the CTV network.

1959 brought the CBC a good deal of grief, much of it self-administered. There had been the Montreal producers' strike, which ended after more than three months with the corporation giving the producers exactly what they'd demanded at the beginning: the right to organize a union. Then in June the CBC enraged the newly re-elected Conservative premier of Ontario, Leslie Frost, by failing to supply lines for him to broadcast a victory speech from his home town, Lindsay, on election night. The CBC's excuse that it wasn't technically feasible to get lines into Lindsay was not well served by a live telecast that same night from the Kitchener, Ontario home of the soundly trounced Ontario

© 1959. Reprinted with permission of the *Toronto Star* Syndicate

"Author! Author!"

The cartoon pistol wielded by Ontario Premier Leslie Frost was less lethal than the legislation drafted later by John Diefenbaker. (Duncan MacPherson in the Toronto Star*)*

Liberal leader, John Wintermeyer. The federal Conservative government of John Diefenbaker took note of their Tory colleagues' cries of political bias; they did nothing to aid the CBC cause in Ottawa.

The snub dealt to Frost wasn't the first situation in which the CBC was perceived by the Conservatives of Canada as a Liberal instrument, and therefore as The Enemy. Back in 1942 CBC radio, under the ham-fisted direction of a new general manager, Dr. J. S. Thompson, had refused to broadcast a speech by retiring Conservative leader, the Right Honourable Arthur Meighen, at the Conservative leadership convention. John Diefenbaker, already a two-year veteran of the House of Commons and a token candidate for the leadership at that convention, could not have failed to note the rebuff, nor to connect it with Mackenzie King's notorious hatred of Meighen, whose acid tongue King had feared in the House of Commons. Diefenbaker had already begun keeping his mental form chart on those "who stood" (friends and allies), and those who didn't (enemies). From 1942

Mackenzie King hated and feared the acid wit and rapier debating style of Arthur Meighen, shown here in a more reflective moment. (Public Archives of Canada)

on there was no question into which column he had consigned the CBC.

In 1959 CBC television was still broadcasting live, with all the attendant delights and horrors that brought. The reminiscences of the period are rich with examples of the hazards of such a system: the folk singer, leaning casually against a mantel while serenading, who trod on his faithful labrador's tail midway through the second chorus, with a predictably disharmonious result; the cute puppy which, during an especially tender love ballad, committed an extremely indelicate act on camera. Often there was only one camera, and hysterical directors were unable to change the shot even in the face of disastrous happenings.

CBC producers hadn't heard of the Billy Rose Broadway stratagem of giving elephants an enema before permitting them on stage, so more than one four-legged TV guest provided critical comment on a programme. One horse endowed a Halifax sound stage around Max Ferguson's feet while his owner (the horse's owner) tried vainly to retrieve something from a nostril with a gnarled finger, and a dog, also part of the visiting group, indulged in some erotic fantasy which left him, in the words of one awed observer, "apparently standing on five legs."

Ferguson, aka Rawhide, played a role in maybe the best dog story of them all during a Christmas Eve broadcast from Halifax. Max's dog, Toughie, had been left to sleep under a sofa on the cosy Christmas set, replete with a cheerful fireplace, a Christmas tree, a costumed Santa and a blazing plum pudding. But at the critical moment in the telecast the bulldog, aroused perhaps by the happy sound of carols, emerged from his resting place, grasped Santa firmly by the left buttock, and continued to gnaw while Santa's plum pudding, propelled into the tree in his shock, set the latter

Max Ferguson (aka Rawhide) waits in a Halifax CBC studio while announcer Don Tremaine reads some copy, and sounds effects engineer Harold Porter prepares his box of tricks; April, 1969. (CBC Archives)

fiercely ablaze. Credits rolled over pictures of the burning Christmas tree, Santa's screeches, and Ferguson's unheeded pleas to Toughie to let go.

The presence of a second camera, even of a third, wasn't always a blessing. My own favourite moment as a viewer came during an early edition of "Cross-Canada Hit Parade" in the fifties. Joyce Hahn, wearing a prim pinafore costume, had just finished a song and the camera cut to her co-star, Wally Koster. But there was a props man carrying a

Joyce Hahn, in a typically inane CBC publicity pose from the fifties. (CBC Archives)

To examine these photos of Wally Koster in sequence is to begin to understand the artificiality necessary in television to simulate reality. (CBC Archives)

stepladder past Koster, so the director opted to cut back to camera one on Miss Hahn. Miss Hahn had already started to leave the set to change for her next number. To facilitate quick changes, she was wearing one of those stage costumes consisting only of a front panel, and tied like an apron under the shoulders, at the waist and hips. Viewers were treated to a rear view of the TV songstress, nude except for three bows across her back and a pair of step-ins. After lingering for a few seconds on Miss Hahn's delectably departing posterior, the director cut back to Wally Koster. Everything in the set was in order, but outside the moonlit window before which Mr. Koster was singing, two more props men walked past, this time with an 18-foot extension ladder.

The on-camera screw-ups were often a respectable metaphor for events behind the scenes, from Parliament Hill and CBC Ottawa's head office to planning headquarters in Toronto. In 1952, for example, Ernie Bushnell had discovered at the penultimate moment that CBLT literally could not be on the air on schedule because there were not enough carpenters, painters and electricians around to finish the studios in time, nor was there any CBC budget to hire more. But there was a budget allocation for freelance "artists," a term used to describe occasional performers. So Bushnell had the needed artisans hired on the artists payroll, and the job got done. Later he was forced to justify himself at a board of directors' meeting. However, he had provided for that very first broadcast from CBLT in Toronto, which included a walk-on bit by actor Don Harron, a song by Wally Koster, some chat by radio's "Mr. Canada," John Fisher, a piano solo by an obscure young fellow named Glenn Gould, and a fainting spell by one unremembered studio cameraman overcome by the pressure of the event.

Drew Crossan, who produced the first CBLT variety show, "Kaleidoscope," on September 8, 1952, was one of several neophyte producers given a six-week cram course in TV production by Rudy Bretz of New York. His classmates included Ross MacLean, Harry Rasky, Norman Jewison, Harvey Hart, even Sydney Newman, who had had some experience as a field producer with NBC. Most of them became household names in the years following: Jewison in New York and Hollywood, Newman first at BBC and then, back in Canada, at the National Film Board. Crossan became CBC's foremost variety producer, a virtually fatal skill, as the corporation worked him relentlessly and, as with more than one colleague, urged him to drive past

"Mr. Canada". John Fisher hosted CBLT's *first-ever telecast in September, 1952. (Ontario Archives: Gilbert W. Milne Collection)*

the limits of physical capacity until his health had been destroyed.

The busiest CBC office in Toronto in 1952 was manned by Eva Langbord, the corporation's highly skilled casting director. As early as June, 1952, 110 female dancers turned out to try for three jobs backing Alan and Blanche Lund on the projected programme, "The Big Revue." One of the audition survivors, the lithe and lovely Lorraine Thompson, later became a TV interviewer and one of the established names in Canadian television.

By the late fifties, CBC had showcased a platoon of toothsome and talented girl singers: Phyllis Marshall, Shirley Harmer, and Joyce Hahn, whose

Early 'cattle calls' for dancers drew Lorraine Thompson (extreme left) out for auditions as producer Norman Campbell pondered the choices. (CBC Archives)

most popular publicity shot revealed the Hit Parade star, or a good deal of her, in a leopard-skin costume. There was Terry Dale, who sang on the very first telecast, and then the public met Joyce Sullivan, Joan Fairfax, the sultry Sylvia Murphy and Herself, Juliette, who even after she began marketing a line of "My Pet" bras amply supported by her own personality and pulchritude, was always too wholesome somehow to really sell a smoky ballad. Her "Good night, mom" sign-off was the benchmark of

Torch singer Sylvia Murphy was probably CBC-TV's sultriest song-stress on "The Music-makers" series. (Private collection: Sylvia Murphy)

her personality. One could admire Juliette's songs and hugely enjoy her tradecraft, but fantasy, especially erotic fantasy, was impossible. Her audiences couldn't make the leap of faith necessary to submerge totally in her music. But even though CBC strove bravely to maintain a goody-two-shoes image for all its actresses and girl singers (a generation later it took Anne Murray a decade to work up the courage to risk her public persona by saying "hell" on a stage), a few smouldered their

Phyllis Marshall began her CBC-TV career in Vancouver. (CBC Archives)

Juliette and her 'Four Romeos'; they were (from the left) Rick Stainsby, Alex Tick, Vern Kennedy and John Garden. (CBC Archives)

As with Oscar Wilde's description of sex, in TV the position was often ridiculous and the pleasure fleeting; this is Sylvia Murphy with stuffed polar bear and close-up camera. (Private collection: Sylvia Murphy)

The longest-running programme on CBC-TV is "Front Page Challenge". This picture, taken in 1962, five years after the series went on the air, has guest panelist Scott Young sandwiched between Betty Kennedy and Pierre Berton, with Gordon Sinclair on the left. (CBC Archives)

way past the ubiquitous glass eye and corporate PR department to permit their viewers some moments of magic and mystery.

The most unreal personalities on early Canadian television were, and often still are, the newsreaders. Announcers chosen for their on-camera presence, the newscasters quickly developed devoted followers who imagined them to be journalists. Some came to believe it themselves, although union

Life wasn't always serious, even in the days before television. Gordon Sinclair interviews beauty contestants at the CNE in 1949. (Ontario Archives: Gilbert W. Milne Collection)

bickering made it impossible, from the beginnings of CBC television, for reporters to write a word of their own copy if they were actually employed to *read* news on the air, or for announcers to function as journalists, even if they possessed the required skills.

CBC's first national newscaster was Larry Henderson, who began on CBLT in 1952. By the late fifties, when Larry signed off his nightly "National News" by saying "Good night," there were literally tens of thousands of Canadians who responded, "Good night, Larry," in the privacy of their livingrooms, and then turned in. Henderson was famous

Larry Henderson —
first voice, and face,
of "The National."
(CBC Archives)

within the CBC for his nightly dash to the men's john for a moment of relief from nervous tension prior to each "National News" telecast. He also became known for jaunts to foreign countries during his annual holidays. He'd return from such trips, festooned in the national dress of that year's country of choice, and deliver talks on the economy and politics of those hapless states on Canada's rubber chicken speaking circuit. After his retirement from CBC, Henderson opened a school for

Earl Cameron. His newscasts were always two days late in Churchill, Manitoba. (CBC Archives)

announcers and hosted frequent foreign tours for the same impressionable folk who had attended his lectures.

The enduring brush war between CBC's reporters and editors on one hand, and its announcers on the other, continued to prevent any rational blend of journalistic skill and news delivery through the end of the seventies. Stanley Burke, whose exemplary (some said foolhardy) courage during the Algerian War won him permanent honour among

Stanley Burke reading the FLQ manifesto on live CBC-TV, October 8, 1970. (Public Archives of Canada)

his colleagues, tried to beat the system as reader of the "National News" in the early seventies. He failed, and retired to a life of good works and public service in British Columbia. Burke's most memorable, as opposed to most notable, TV moment came in the sixties, when he was hosting a news special. A confused director or control room switcher cut the cameras back to Burke instead of going to another studio location to pick up a commentary from another reporter. Burke, clearly unaware he was on camera, let alone that his microphone was also live, glared off camera for a few timeless seconds at an equally frustrated studio director, who was evidently motioning him to resume his commentary — any commentary. "Jesus Christ," snarled the usually suave and impeccably correct Burke, "don't cue me *now*!" Canada's TV screens went momentarily to black.

American TV networks avoided the internecine warfare that hamstrung the CBC news service. As a result, in the late seventies after a brief reprise of Stanley Burke's experience, another gifted, professional CBC correspondent, Peter Kent, left the crown corporation for sunnier prospects south of the border. Attrition, one might say of the corporation, was its greatest product.

One perverse effect of the dichotomy between news reporters and news hosts was a gradual loss of credibility in newscasts for TV viewers. The union struggle over CBC television news operations gradually had the effect of enhancing the appeal and impact of the so-called "public affairs" shows. Starting with Ross MacLean's "Tabloid" and "701" programmes, and continuing through such series as "Document," produced by Douglas Leiterman, and "Inquir'y," produced by Patrick Watson, the public developed a loyalty to current affairs personalities who went on location to get the stories,

CBC correspondents at play. In the back row, left to right: Stanley Burke, Knowlton Nash, James M. Minifie (who is pulling at his glass eye), and Norman DePoe. In the front row: Michael Maclear, Tom Gould and Phil Calder. (Public Archives of Canada)

and then delivered those stories in studio, often with appropriate studio interviews. Charles Templeton and others were roving the globe, shooting film interviews with pioneer TV cameramen like Bob Crone, and then introducing their own stories on Canadian TV, while Larry Henderson was wearing Middle Eastern robes to Rotary Club luncheons.

The public began noticing the difference, much to the chagrin of news department employees. The guy who'd been in the field obviously had more persuasive clout than the fellow who'd strolled to the news studio from the announcer's lounge at 354 Jarvis Street in Toronto. Worse, maybe, in the long term, those public affairs reporters were able to gather far wider experience and a much fuller variety of skills than most news reporters. Normally the public affairs types, less burdened by union caveats, doubled as researchers, film directors, interviewers, reporters, and finally as on-camera hosts of their own stories and programmes. As a result, CBC television news became a sort of Canadian almanac of daily events, regarded as utterly dependable, and largely grey if not sterile. But the much looser, more raunchy public affairs shows captured more attention and became ground zero for much of the controversy swirling about the aching heads of CBC head office brass in Ottawa.

"This Hour Has Seven Crises": 1964-1966

But it was "This Hour Has Seven Days" that capped the inexorable march of public affairs programming into the most tender parts of the Canadian psyche. It was the invention of Douglas Leiterman and Patrick Watson, after two years of conversation and planning, and with the essential support, advice and succor of CBC public affairs executives like Reeves Haggen and Bernard Ostry (later Canada's undersecretary of state and later still deputy minister of federal communications). The programme, which created more furor than any CBC programme before or since, was a natural extension of Leiterman's "Document" series and Watson's "Inquir'y" programmes from Ottawa. It was also an organic extension of the belief shared by both men (both graduate students of Ross MacLean's TV philosophy, which they had learned as his proteges and acolytes) that public affairs could be made vital, arresting, provocative and relevant to all Canadians, whether their TV tastes ran to NHL hockey or Nathan Cohen's erudite panel shows.

There is a delicious footnote to the "Seven Days" controversy in which, as a story editor, film director, writer and interviewer for the "Inquir'y" series, I had a peripheral part. In the spring of 1963 Davidson Dunton, who was studio host of the series, was appointed to the Bilingualism and Biculturalism Commission by Prime Minister

Pearson. With the former chairman of CBC lost as a host, Patrick Watson began casting about that summer for a new host to begin the fall TV season, and came up with the notion that we should employ a Francophone in that role — a very daring departure for the English-language CBC. Viewers were still smarting from the early experiments in bilingual television when, for example, sportscasters would broadcast the play-by-play portions of a football game in one language, and offer between-plays commentary in the other. In any event, Patrick heard of a bright young professor at the University of Montreal who was fluently bilingual and might be the right man for the job.

After a couple of conversations the law professor conceded some interest in the notion, and agreed to do a couple of political interviews with the two-man interview technique we had been developing in the "Inquir'y" series (later characterized by critics, not always in a flattering way, as the "hotseat" interview). Arrangements were completed, the professor was briefed, and a pair of audition interviews were videotaped in a Montreal studio. One of them was with Claude Wagner, then justice minister in the government of Quebec Premier Jean Lesage, later both a leadership candidate and, because of a trust fund established to guarantee his solvency in Ottawa, an embarrassment to the federal Progressive Conservative Party. The interviews, which were telecast, were terrific. The professor was a natural, and he was pressed to take the job.

But hosting "Inquir'y" required his presence in Ottawa every Monday throughout the winter. After reflection the candidate, Professor Pierre Elliot Trudeau, decided the TV job might interfere unduly with ski weekends in the Laurentians, and he declined. At this point Patrick Watson and I met another Francophone academic, a professor at McGill of Canadian history. His name was Laurier LaPierre and he, too, was a natural. Soon Laurier and I were sharing the two-man interview chores he later continued with Patrick and others. In 1964 we all went on to help create and broadcast "Seven Days." It wasn't until 1965 that Trudeau decided to move to Ottawa after all, as the Liberal MP for Mount Royal. But would CBC's history, and Canada's, have been different if the law professor had hosted "Inquir'y" and, subsequently, "This Hour Has Seven Days?"

Bernard Ostry who, as deputy minister of the Department of Communications in Ottawa, finally gave Canadian communications researchers the support and credit they needed to achieve major successes. (Government of Canada)

"Seven Days" has now attained the status of legend in Canadian broadcasting, a nostalgic and unattainable Oz floating somewhere just out of the sight and reach of all who labour to make TV exciting and gripping to a national audience. Part of the programme's genesis lay in the news/public affairs dichotomy described earlier; without it, Douglas Leiterman would probably have become a CBC news producer and correspondent. Leiterman was a former Nieman fellow and, like many of us, a retreaded newspaperman. Overlaying every aspect of "Seven Days" was the prodigious creative energy

Roy Faibish: endow-ed with a puckish wit, a taste for Arlo Guth-rie and James Joyce, and an incisive gift for divining the politic-ally possible. (Govern-ment of Canada)

of Watson and Leiterman, and their extraordinary
capacity to generate and maintain astonishing
loyalty and effort. There were, as well, the finely
tuned political and administrative gifts of men like
Ostry, Haggen and Roy Faibish (who went on to
administer Ernie Bushnell's private TV empire in
Ottawa in the late sixties with Stuart Griffiths,
and in the seventies was a commissioner of the
Canadian Radio-Television Commission). Above all,
there was the huge audience appetite, tested by
those earlier programme series, for television with
some relevance, some irony and some bite. The

Stuart Griffiths. He built 32-foot yachts by hand in Ernie Bushnell's studios in Ottawa, and gave the capital city some of Canada's best television. Judy LaMarsh wanted him as CBC president in 1966. (Government of Canada)

standard television procession of the bland leading the bland no longer had even novelty to recommend it.

"Seven Days" was cheeky, irreverent, boisterous and, occasionally, savage or pompous — as are, always, idealism, conviction, and the acts of those with A Cause. Our case was felt to be righteous in direct proportion to outraged attacks from politicians and the pressures generated by CBC head office. By its end "Seven Days" was like the operations shack on an RAF fighter airfield during the Battle of Britain: tense, with unpredictable bursts of temperament; beleaguered, but mostly suffused with indomitable camaraderie, unity of purpose, and resolve to stay in the air until every gun platform was shot from under us. Like the Spitfires of Word War II, of course, "Seven Days" programmes, if televised today, would seem more quaint than impressive.

There were other parallels. One "Seven Days" researcher, C. Alexander Brown, did a casual clipboard survey of our staff of 40-odd during the second (and final) year of the series and found all of us, but three, had at least six of the classic symptoms of battle fatigue. Those three subsequently left television. And, like Spitfire pilots and crews, "Seven Days" staff frequently exceeded the stress specification limits of their vehicle. Most of the excesses were those of conviction and dedication. Few "Seven Days" segments could have been characterized as irresponsible, least of all the one which brought an inadvertent tear to Laurier LaPierre's cheek when he first saw on his monitor, during a live, Sunday night show, a moving interview about an arguably wrongfully convicted youth serving a life term for murder. That tear was seized on by then CBC President Alphonse Ouimet as evidence of "hysterical and emotional" irresponsi-

C. Alexander Brown (right) with the author on the set of "The Public Eye", 1967. (Globe & Mail, Toronto)

bility. It was, in fact, evidence only of humanity, not a bad failing in a TV journalist or host.

Another bum rap accorded "Seven Days" came when, after a taped interview was edited and telecast, McGeorge Bundy, of the Kennedy establishment but at that time a Lyndon Johnson satrap, sent Canadian daily newspapers a printed, marked transcript of both the original, uncut interview and of the version telecast by "Seven Days." It was clear from Bundy's transcript, published in many newspapers, that he had been grossly misrepresented via distortions caused by vicious and dishonest editing. What the newspapers did not know was that it was Bundy's transcript that had been doctored before being mailed from the White House.

The "Seven Days" edit had been entirely fair, even-handed and representative. Sadly, many of the newspapers to which we sent data on the 30 or more deliberate misstatements of fact in Bundy's document published his material but not ours. So easily may a suspicion of irresponsibility be fanned into a conviction.

"Seven Days" was not, on reflection, ever guilty of deliberate distortion or journalistic irresponsibility. It *was* occasionally guilty of bad taste, most notably after the recruitment of Robert Emmit Hoyt, a swash-and-buckle American para-journalist hired in Washington by Leiterman. In the second year of "Seven Days," Hoyt became *de facto* producer of every second programme. His first noticeable contribution to "Seven Days," a conspicuous demonstration of his journalistic technique, was a film essay on Walter Jenkins, the tragic, homosexual aide to Lyndon Johnson who'd been abandoned by the leader for whom he'd sacrificed his personal and working life. Hoyt's "sympathetic" description of Jenkins' woes had included a "subjective camera" descent into the public washroom in Washington in which Jenkins had been arrested for a morals offense.

On the plus side, "Seven Days" had made hard-nosed political interviews respectable, and had exposed venality and inhumanity in the treatment of scores of Canadians. The programme had forced every other agency of journalism in the nation to see to its laurels, its energy and its imagination. And it *had* proved that more people could be attracted to public affairs television than to NHL hockey.

Finally, "Seven Days" producers grew incurably weary of CBC head office interference with stories. In fact, many of the best stories developed in the second year of "Seven Days" were never telecast.

Head office, for its part, developed a zero pain threshold after two years of being badgered by Ottawa politicians and mandarins demanding to know why *they* were being pilloried.

No one should ever expect politicians to play fairly. Example: One evening, after an acerbic, live television interview by Laurier LaPierre and myself, John Diefenbaker told us in the studio he'd never had a more stimulating and enjoyable time. "But tomorrow," said Laurier, "your colleagues will be protesting that we weren't kind to you." The Chief was shocked by the suggestion. "You send them to me," he said. "I won't tolerate that sort of interference. It's been a fine interview. Fine." The next day, persuaded by some of those colleagues that he'd not done too well in presenting his case on the programme, Diefenbaker rose in the House of Commons to denounce the badgering, harassment and generally unfair and irresponsible treatment he'd been accorded on Canada's national TV network.

With neither the "Seven Days" staff nor the CBC head office willing to take yes for an answer, the death of the show was certain at the end of the second season. Alphonse Ouimet probably sealed the casket the day he told the "Seven Days" staff at a Toronto meeting that, "of course" creative personnel were interchangeable in the same fashion as the electronic components of his youth. It was that gut conviction from the man who generally ignored programming in his tenure as CBC president, while lugging his organizational chart covered with coloured strings and elastic bands — so he could rearrange administrative lines of authority whenever things seemed not to be running efficiently — to meetings in the CBC regions, which finally ended "Seven Days," and with it an incandescent flare over the TV wasteland.

Alphonse Ouimet claimed from the beginning that CBC management wanted only (a) to separate Leiterman, LaPierre and Watson, whom they saw as a mutually supportive group of Peck's Bad Boys, and (b) to end the situation in which the co-producer (Watson) also hosted his own show. The "Seven Days" response was that, by contract and tradition, producers (Leiterman and Watson) had an inalienable right to select whomever they wished (Watson) as host. But the real dispute lay simply in the fact that CBC brass were made acutely and chronically uncomfortable by the "Seven Days" programme. It was nice — nice, hell, it was marvellous — to win international awards with Norman Campbell's magnificent drama and ballet productions. (Campbell was a judge at those first auditions for dancers in 1952.) But it was unbearable to build audience ratings and national acclaim over the prostrate forms of beleaguered CBC head office personnel who were fearful of attending Ottawa cocktail parties where they might be assaulted by furious cabinet ministers and assorted mandarins.

Moreover, other people (chiefly news personnel) within CBC were grumbling about the high profile and profligate style of the new kid on the block. At one point the ludicrous, intra-departmental tension reached such levels that, frustrated by a refusal from CBC television news to release an archival film clip wanted for a "Seven Days" broadcast, a "Seven Days" staffer stole the film one dark night from the news library.

On the "Seven Days" side, there was an equally profound mistrust of CBC vice-presidents, who were perceived as having no interest or sympathy whatsoever in journalism or programming. Ouimet was seen chiefly, if not exclusively, as concerned with moving elastic bands around on his organiza-

Laurier LaPierre and Patrick Watson – Alphonse Ouimet's vision of Peck's Bad Boys – on the set of "This Hour Has Seven Days," 1966. (CBC Archives)

tional board, and with shuffling the human components of his empire from one programme bin to another, irrespective of personality, creative suitability or desire. Toronto CBC producers threatened to strike, the public wrote letters to their MP's, and viewers picketed the CBC building on Jarvis Street. But the final credits for "Seven Days" had started rolling at corporation headquarters in Ottawa months before the end. The orgies of emotion from SRO studio audiences in Toronto those last few Sunday nights were more in the nature of a wake than a defiant gesture.

Prime Minister Pearson found the perfect diplomat's solution. Faced by a parliamentary committee enquiry into the sorry mess, he appointed

Viewers protesting the CBC head office decision to remove Patrick Watson from "Seven Days." The programme got three to four thousand letters weekly during its final month on the air. (CBC Archives)

Stuart Keate, a respected Vancouver publisher, to arbitrate the dispute. His gesture was much like applying a tourniquet to a corpse. "Seven Days" was already dead, its staff scattered, its high hopes and excitement already rusting on the scrap heap of half-realized dreams.

As for, "Why hasn't there been anything like that, since then?"

Well, Virginia, first, nothing real could ever match the larger-than-life-sized memory. Second, the habit of tough, investigative journalism is now at least partially entrenched in all of Canada's reporting media; and because it's no longer the novelty it was during "Seven Days," it has less glamour. Third, B. F. Skinner was right: negative conditioning is a powerful instrument. The succeeding generations of CBC bureaucrats and producers have mostly learned not to rock the boat hard enough to splash the poop deck. Finally, Virginia, television is hardly ever live anymore, and without the live telecasts that came out of CBC's Studio One in Toronto in those halcyon and heady days of the mid-sixties, there just can't ever be the urgency and excitement necessary to strike synchronous sparks in the audience.

But "Seven Days" left a rich legacy:

a) audiences who know now that news needn't be the "radio with pictures" that was CBC television's first mandate and inclination.

b) a certain knowledge among pompous and lazy journalists that some pushy newcomer may swing in out of left field and tear their heads off, exposing their lack of wit and imagination at a press conference or in coverage of an election campaign.

c) major revisions in law that make it almost impossible in Canada for a person to be ruthlessly and improperly committed to a mental hospital indefinitely — that after the "Seven Days" ex-posé of the Fred Fawcett case, a story obtained by a researcher, Michael Hastings, who smuggled a film camera in a wicker picnic basket into the hospital where Fawcett was being held. Cheeky? Certainly. But effective? You bet.

d) several hundred Canadians who are alive today thanks to artificial kidney machines. Before the "Seven Days" story on the death lottery among such patients, 300 people died annually for want of equipment available in this country to fewer than 50 patients.

By Roy Peterson

"I hope it will always be the policy of federal governments not to interfere with the programming of the CBC." — Hon. Maurice Lamontagne, quoting government policy in Parliament

Few believed Ottawa protestations of virtue and denials of political interference with CBC *in the Pearson years. (MacLean's Magazine: December 2, 1964)*

e) Canadian politicians who have learned that sometimes they will be called to account when they tell lies. Whether through the satiric songs of Dinah Christie or the crisp interviews of Patrick Watson *et confrères*, "Seven Days" did as much as any single journalistic institution to revive that flagging perception in Canada.

Not a bad track record. And not a bad epitaph.

Private Television; The Spoils of Victory: 1948-1959

When television came to Canada in 1952, the CBC was still both participant and arbiter of broadcasting across the country. It was a firm policy of government that any national broadcasting service was to be provided by the crown corporation, and that use of radio and TV channels by private broadcasters was, at best, a privilege. Private broadcasters were on the air on sufferance, as a supplement to the national system. If they happened to make some profit from that system it was ok; but they had no inherent right to use the limited broadcast frequencies. No government ever re-cast that policy in formal terms, but it was to be radically altered in 1958 by the Diefenbaker government. After that year private station operators always believed their licences were a matter of right, and that they were the competitors, not the helpers, of the national network service.

In the beginning it was agreed that CBC should establish TV stations in major Canadian cities, and that private licences should be offered in other cities where financing made it impossible for the CBC to meet the capital costs of establishing service. No second stations were to be licenced until every city had a TV service. Though it was never formally described, that initial plan was for CBC to build stations in every provincial capital city. Affiliate services could then be provided to private stations in other communities. CBC began with Toronto and

Montreal, added Ottawa, and by 1955, having abandoned the abortive, bilingual broadcast effort, added French-language TV in Ottawa and Montreal as well as a fourth and fifth English station in Winnipeg and Vancouver.

That same year, 1955, private stations were on the air in the following cities: St. John's, Newfoundland; Saint John and Moncton, New Brunswick; Hamilton, Kitchener, London, Windsor, Wingham, Barrie, Sudbury, Sault Ste. Marie and Port Arthur, Ontario; Brandon, Manitoba; Saskatoon and Regina, Saskatchewan; Lethbridge, Edmonton and Calgary, Alberta. Private licences had also been approved for Timmins and North Bay, Ontario, as well as for Charlottetown, Prince Edward Island and Jonquiere and Sherbrooke, Quebec. By Dominion Day of 1958 there were 50 TV stations operating in Canada, only eight of them owned by the CBC. So within three years of Percy Saltzman's first appearance on CBLT Toronto, a government policy of giving CBC stations priority in major cities across Canada was already in tatters, the victim of a failure by government to fund the corporation adequately. By 1955, five of Canada's provinces were being serviced exclusively by private stations.

Network facilities, too, were slow in coming. In 1953 a microwave link was completed between Toronto, Montreal and Ottawa, but national microwave wasn't ready until 1958. In August, 1954, when there were 800,000 TV sets in Canada, CBC telecast live coverage of Roger Bannister's "miracle mile" from the Vancouver Commonwealth Games by borrowing American facilities to feed the programme to eastern Canada. Three years later in November, 1957, CBC again had to lease American facilities to telecast the Grey Cup game to Vancouver from Toronto.

From the beginning, royal commissions and

parliamentary committees had recommended that the CBC be given statutory, long-term financing, based, for example, on a percentage of gross national product, or on the number of radio/TV sets in the country. But unlike BBC, which is given funding for five-year periods, CBC always had to approach parliament, cap in hand, for annual allocations. Thus hamstrung, the corporation never successfully did any long-term programme or capital planning. All was *ad hoc*, hand to mouth.

Examples of the consequences of this lack of proper budget planning still exist. Since capital is always in short supply, and given the geographic demands to extend coverage, CBC production units are rarely permitted to spend money on purchases, although rentals, often more expensive, are permitted. One frustrated producer arranged to rent a $2,000 tape recorder from a private supplier with a personal undertaking that, after the original purchase cost plus an adequate profit had been paid by way of rentals, the supplier would write off the machine and take it off his books. The CBC thus acquired a tape recorder and the rental fees ended after less than a year. However, when the programme series ended, the machine, which did not exist in anyone's books, clearly couldn't be kept by the CBC. So the phantom unit disappeared, and a short-sighted federal funding policy, coupled with CBC's usual bureaucratic astigmatism, resulted in Canadian taxpayers and TV viewers losing a valuable piece of equipment. That sample event could almost certainly be multiplied by a factor of several thousand.

The first private applications for TV licences, six of them, arrived before the board of governors of the CBC in October, 1948. The government wasn't ready. By 1949 the administration headed by Prime Minister Louis St. Laurent was ready to announce an interim policy. The CBC would be expected to build stations in Montreal and Ottawa, and to provide programming material to private stations in other cities. A month later the government appointed another royal commission. The Massey Commission into "National Development in the Arts, Letters and Sciences," was named on April 8, 1949. It did not report until May 13, 1951. The first task assigned to the commission was to "examine and make recommendations upon the principles upon which the policy of Canada should be based, in the fields of radio and television broadcasting."

The commission recommended that the CBC continue as the regulator of Canadian broadcasting; that no private stations be licenced until CBC had developed national programmes; that all private stations be required to carry "national programmes;" that Canadian talent be encouraged and excessive commercialism be curbed; and that yet another "independent body" re-examine the whole business within three years of the start of Canadian TV.

With no videotape and no microwave network facilities, CBC had to distribute its national programming via filmed copies of its live programmes, called kinescopes. These film copies of programmes, made by 16mm film cameras shooting a green-coloured TV monitor, produced, at best, dark prints of the original programmes, with muddy optical film soundtracks. However, the "snow" and other interference on TV sets in the fifties covered a multitude of shortcomings. The upshot was that by 1954 CBC was buying and using about 40 million feet of 16mm film each year — in other words, 4,000 *miles* of film.

Until the final installation of satellite relays in the 1970's, kine recordings were still used to relay broadcasts to many remote areas in Canada. In Churchill, Manitoba, for example, viewers of the

one-room TV station, housed in a clapboard government building on the harbour, regularly saw
Earl Cameron's "National News" 24 hours after the
event, when a kine of the programme arrived on
the daily DC-3 Trans-Air flight from Winnipeg,
connecting with Toronto. However, there were no
weekend flights, so Monday was catch-up day, with
Earl evidently reading the Friday, Saturday and
Sunday night newscasts back to back. When
weather grounded the Trans-Air flights, Churchill
simply didn't get the news and had to make do,
instead, with a library of old Groucho Marx films.

There were advantages to *ad hoc* community
operations like Churchill's TV station. If a viewer
missed an item on the "National News," he could
always call Lorne, the station's accountant/technical
operator/manager/announcer and writer, who lived
and slept in a small room next door to the 20-foot
square studio, and ask for a repeat telecast. Lorne
would obligingly thread up the CBC newscast from
several days earlier and call the viewer to let him
know what time it would be rebroadcast.

On December 2, 1955, faithful to the Massey
Commission's request, the federal government
appointed a brand-new royal commission to "examine and make recommendations upon certain
matters related to sound and television broadcasting in Canada." This commission, headed by Robert
Fowler, took 16 months to bring in its report on
March 15, 1957, just three months before John
Diefenbaker's election as the first Conservative
prime minister of Canada in more than two decades.

Fowler recommended creation of an independent "board of broadcast governors" with regulatory
authority over Canadian broadcasting but without
licencing powers. He also urged long-term, statutory
funding of CBC and, maybe most fatally, urged the

CBC to plunge more heavily into commercial sales. Noting that "advertising is a positive contributor to living standards and economic activity and should not be regarded as ... regrettable," Fowler went on to conclude that "when the CBC is engaged in commercial activities, it should do so vigorously and with the objective of earning the maximum revenue from those activities."

That policy, happily used by successive federal governments to truncate Ottawa funding of the national broadcasting organization, contributed to the worst features of CBC television and prevented the best being realized. Examples:

a) Forced to compete for commercial dollars with private TV stations, the CBC frequently opted for lowest-common-denominator programming in prime time, usually via American "situation" TV series.

b) Very considerable sums of public money were wasted in bidding wars between CBC and private broadcasters for the rights to American or British TV shows, or for the rights to Canadian sporting events such as NHL hockey and Canadian Football League games, especially telecasts of the finals and of the Grey Cup. The only beneficiaries of these "auctions" were the club owners and the advertising agencies.

c) Since advertising rates in television, like those in newspapers and magazines, are based on circulation, CBC was forced to court high ratings at the expense of programming better suited to the purposes of the country and the corporation. Those pressures clearly contributed, through the late sixties and early seventies, to a decline in experimental variety and drama productions at CBC which came close to entirely eliminating that area of Canadian television.

With the development of cable TV which brought

multiple-choice viewing to the vast majority of Canadian homes, the business of playing ratings numbers games under the obligation to produce commercial revenue made even less sense. But the Fowler Commission, while happily endorsing the policy goals of CBC President Davie Dunton, failed to realized the paradox in supporting his policies while making them impossible to attain. Dunton had been approvingly quoted by the commission in his conviction that:

"The Canadian Broadcasting Corporation is charged...to develop the best possible service of *Canadian programs*...to enrich the lives of individual Canadians with all their diversity of interests. At the same time, it should stimulate the life of the nation in many ways; by offering opportunities for the artistic and creative and communicative abilities of Canadians to develop and to be appreciated and shared in by other Canadians...by also giving people opportunities for some new insights and understandings; by helping Canadians to know and understand one another and to know other parts of their own country better; by reflecting the diverse traditions that make up the Canadian heritage; by meeting and stimulating the interests of Canadians in other Canadians and in the achievements, ideas and creative work of other peoples, all in the one Canadian spirit."

Robert Fowler, like Vincent Massey before him, also took time to criticize the CBC for failure to enforce its own broadcast regulations with enough vigour, and for failure to keep the public sufficiently informed of corporation policy and operations. He missed the point that many CBC policies were purely a matter of spasm response and crisis management, given the year-to-year imperatives of 12-month-only funding.

Fowler urged against acceptance of the Canadian Broadcasters' Association recommendation for creation of an independent board of broadcast governors for Canada to control *all* aspects of broadcasting, but that was before the election of the Diefenbaker government. When John Diefenbaker was returned with the largest parliamentary majority in Canadian history on March 31, 1958, he was politically muscled for just about anything he wanted to do — and he wanted to clip the CBC's wings. Fowler had argued for an independent regulatory tribunal, but he wanted a continuing role for CBC as the agency for licencing Canadian broadcasting. The Tories disagreed.

Three months after John Diefenbaker's triumphal return to Parliament Hill came the humiliating CBC snub of Ontario Premier Leslie Frost. Nor had the new prime minister forgotten Arthur Meighen. A month later, on July 1, 1958 Davie Dunton resigned as chairman of the CBC. At that point events seemed to accelerate. On November 1 the government proclaimed Canada's new Broadcast Act, over the bitter opposition of Mike Pearson's rump group of Liberal opposition MP's. That same day Tory Secretary of State George Nowlan appointed Alphonse Ouimet as president of the CBC, with Ernie Bushnell as vice-president and assistant general manager. Ouimet celebrated by leaving for a Florida vacation immediately after his installation on December 8, and the hapless Bushnell was left to face the Montreal producers' strike a few days later.

Bushnell's authority and freedom of movement at CBC had been threatened from the day "Al" Ouimet became president. By September, 1959 the new president, still fiddling with his organizational charts, had decided to enhance his own authority by watering down that of everyone under him. His method was to create a whole series of extra vice-presidencies, and to avoid confrontation he ordered Ernie Bushnell to stay away from the board meeting at which this recommendation was rubber stamped. By the time of the "Seven Days" fiasco in 1965-66, Ouimet had nine vice-presidents, at least two of whom, Bud Walker and Captain W.E.S. Briggs, were directly responsible for much of the employee disaffection within CBC.

In her political memoirs, Judy LaMarsh, secretary of state from December, 1965 until the 1968 general election, describes how, after she vetoed Briggs' re-appointment as a vice-president in 1967, Ouimet arranged to have the doughty captain revert, *pro forma*, to his "employee" status from that of an "appointee," and thereby receive a sharply increased pension together with a full year's salary as a retirement bonus. Bud Walker's punishment for having done more than any other CBC administrator to exacerbate employee-head office relations was, the summer after the "Seven Days" crisis, a two-year appointment as an advisor on radio/television development in the Caribbean Islands within the Commonwealth, based in Jamaica. Miss LaMarsh says of Alphonse Ouimet, "He had the perfect temperament of the research engineer...He had a positive passion for organization charts, and none at all for the people they represented."

At the end of 1967, having fought the feisty Miss LaMarsh and lost, Alphonse Ouimet resigned. He was succeeded, not by the brilliant broadcaster Stuart Griffiths whom Judy LaMarsh had urged on Prime Minister Pearson, but by a man chosen by Pearson to keep the lid on, former treasury board secretary, George Davidson. Miss LaMarsh considered Davidson "a highly skilled and intelligent member of the public service. However," she added, "I do not know of a single talent which he possessed which fitted my concept of what the Corporation urgently needed, other than the fact that he was bilingual." Certainly George Davidson, a civilized and decent man, showed himself well suited to presiding over the decline of imagination, enthusiasm and creativity within CBC during his years in office.

John Diefenbaker's appointments to his new Board of Broadcast Governors, like his new Broadcast Act, amplified his view that it was "our turn" in a Tory-operated national capital. The Chief was firmly convinced that three royal commissions and sixteen parliamentary committees had been wrong, and that the CBC should be taken out of the business of licencing broadcasting stations, as it had clearly been an instrument of the Liberals. Radio and TV licences had been, said Diefenbaker in his political memoirs, "a Liberal Party licence to print money, aided and abetted by . . . intellectual and artistic 'dumping' from the United States." Moreover, he added:

"The CBC was as much to blame as the private stations. It may be the essential truth that the CBC had become so indoctrinated with the Liberal viewpoint that it indiscriminately embraced North American continentalism and could not differentiate, its academic and intellectual pretenses to the contrary, between American national opinion and true internationalism. It was therefore important that national broadcasting policy be regulated by a body responsible to Parliament . . . [a] Board truly representative of all areas and sectors of the nation."

The proof that pudding came in the appointments. There were to be three permanent members of the new Board of Broadcast Governors: a chairman, Dr. Andrew Stewart, president of the University of Alberta and a political economist; a vice-chairman, Quebec Tory enthusiast Roger

© 1959. Reprinted with permission of the *Toronto Star* Syndicate

ACTING CBC PRESIDENT
E.L. BUSHNELL — "WHEN I
LEAVE, I'LL BE FIRED."

Calling The Shot

The aftermath of the producers' strike in 1959; the federal cabinet joined Alphonse Ouimet in the bunkers while Ernie Bushnell faced the heavy artillery. (Duncan MacPherson in the Toronto Star*)*

Duhamel; and Carlyle Allison, described by Diefenbaker as "a nationally known newspaperman from Winnipeg." The prime minister could have added the words "ardent Tory supporter and close personal friend," but did not.

Other board members included a brother-in-law of Diefenbaker's cabinet colleague, George Hees; the Diefenbaker family's Prince Albert dentist; a failed Tory candidate from New Brunswick; a former secretary of the Progressive Conservative Association of Nova Scotia; a former leader of the P.C. Association of Newfoundland, and a Conservative Party worker from Montreal. There certainly weren't going to be any more "Liberal Party licences to print money" by way of broadcast licences from the new Board of Broadcast Governors.

At the end of 1959, with both Alphonse Ouimet and the Board of Broadcast Governors firmly in place, Ernie Bushnell resigned from the CBC and was replaced by Captain W. E. S. Briggs. In January, 1960 the BBG opened its hearings to consider applications for second TV station licences in Canada's eight major cities. So began the most promising decade of Canadian television, as licence applicants promised everything from grand opera to repertory drama companies in their scramble to get one of those "licences to print money."

The Private Networks; Doing Well Versus Doing Good: 1960-1980

By the time the Board of Broadcast Governors invited applicants to submit reasons why they should be granted TV licences in the eight major cities selected for second TV stations, the Canadian television industry had already become a major factor in the Canadian economy. By the end of 1959 Canadians had bought more than 3.5 million television sets; the purchase cost alone of sets in Canadian homes was approaching the $2 billion mark. Since 1936 when it had 132 employees, the CBC had swollen to encompass over 7,000 staffers, including those extra vice-presidents.

Competition for the new TV licences in Canada's largest commercial markets (Halifax, Montreal, Ottawa, Toronto, Winnipeg, Edmonton, Calgary and Vancouver) was fierce to the point of barbarity. Applicants foreshadowed a television perfume commercial of later years with their approach to the BBG of "promise them anything." But few neglected, either, to include some prominent Progressive Conservative allies, supporters, organizers or bagmen on their putative boards of directors. CBC, embarrassed by its absence from all of prairie Canada except Winnipeg, applied for and received the second licence for Edmonton, over the strenuous complaints of several other local applicants.

Ernie Bushnell went after the second Ottawa licence and was on the air in that city on March 10, 1961. But he was beaten to the airwaves by the first private station in Montreal, CFCF-TV, which began telecasts on January 20 of that year. Both were latecomers to the "new boys'" club headed then, as for a generation to come, by John F. Bassett, whose CFTO Toronto celebrated New Year's Day, 1961 with its inaugural broadcast. CBC, rarely less than lethargic in corporate development, didn't televise to Edmontonians until October 2, 1961.

By the end of 1961 Canada had 64 television stations and 26 satellite "repeater" stations. The CBC staff rolls were up to 8,000 and the corporation estimated that 94 per cent of Canadians were within reach of either its English or French TV networks. Radio was also extended, beginning with the creation of a CBC fm network in 1960, and the development of a regional northern radio network to supplement short-wave service to the Yukon and Northwest Territories. Anyone eyeing the lucrative TV marketplace in the eight years during which Canadians bought 3.5 million TV sets, generally failed to notice that they also purchased another 3.2 million radios. Just as radio had not replaced newspapers, so TV was far from killing radio.

The problem was simply that TV was more exciting, more ostentatious and, from the beginning, more wealthy. For example, in 1958 CBC bought 3,857 radio scripts and only 1,213 TV scripts, but paid more than twice as much — $8.5 million — for TV writing and performing than for radio work, which generated only $4 million for the writers and performers of the senior service. So with three times the volume of work producing only half the income, it was no wonder Canada's artistic community was beating down the doors of TV casting offices.

As early as 1955 the CBC had already lost its domination of Canadian broadcasting. The Massey

Commission had made it clear that no private TV stations should be licenced until the CBC had established a truly national service, but the government, despite assurances to the contrary, had permitted licencing of private stations in six provincial capitals ahead of the CBC. The notion of electronic communications as a national trust and utility was moribund.

Diefenbaker had told parliament back in February, 1945 that the CBC had no right to be "both a cop and a competitor...both litigant and judge, both investigator and jury." He now made certain it wasn't. The prime minister poured acid into the wound when he took the occasion of the CBC's 25th anniversary (November 2, 1961) to announce that the new Broadcast Act brought "order...out of confusion and complaint...between public and private systems." Brushing aside Mike Pearson's ineffectual parliamentary opposition, and ignoring the Massey and Fowler recommendations for five-year grants, John Diefenbaker had rushed the Broadcast Act from first reading to royal assent in just 18 days in August and September, 1958.

Even out of power the Conservative Party continued to frustrate rational financing of the public broadcast service. In her new Broadcast Act of 1968, Judy LaMarsh built in a clause of statutory, five-year financing of CBC. But under fierce attack from the Conservative members of parliament, the section was removed in a political trade-off.

Of all the new, big-city licencees given TV launch pads in 1960, Ernie Bushnell had clearly demonstrated the most imagination and concern for responsible broadcasting. Together with Stuart Griffiths, he set out to build the best broadcast service possible without government subsidy. For a few heady years, fuelled by the creative energy of men like Roy Faibish and Peter Reilly, Canada's most brilliant and fiery television journalist, Bushnell and Griffiths came close to achieving their goal. Griffiths, who'd been Bushnell's chief aide in getting CBLT on the air back in 1952, had returned to Canada after a five-year stint as a programme manager at Granada TV in Britain only to fail in his bid for the Toronto TV licence. He then agreed to join Bushnell in his application. Peter Reilly, who later served a term as an MP for a west Ottawa riding, died tragically in 1976, a victim of the pressures of 25 years on television, of booze, and in his mid-forties, of the cheap carping of critics unable to perceive his extraordinary gifts and dedication to his viewers and to his craft.

But everyone knew that Toronto was the mother lode, the real bonanza of the 1960's claim race for TV licences. Nor did many express shock over Griffiths' loss at the Toronto hearings. Although there were nine Toronto applicants, one of them, John F. Bassett, publisher of the *Toronto Telegram*, had bought a $132,000 parcel of land for his studio and had the blueprints drawn even before the licence hearings. Bassett had told friends his application was "in the bag," and so had his close personal friend, George Hees, a senior member of the Diefenbaker cabinet and, you'll recall, brother-in-law of a member of the BBG. After the event, when the Tory publisher and his associates had their licence for CFTO-TV, both Hees and Diefenbaker bragged to friends that they had helped with the decision. Hees actually told an interviewer, in a recorded session, that he had been "very helpful to him (Bassett) in getting his television licence."

In a tidy example of reciprocity, Bassett's *Telegram* heaped flattery on Hees; this most conspicuously when the former minister of trade and commerce returned to the hustings in the 1965 election campaign after having dropped out of the House of Commons in 1963, disheartened by his failed attempt to play Brutus to John Diefenbaker's Caesar. When the two men appeared together on a platform in Hees' Northumberland riding in 1965, *Telegram* reporter Ron Collister wrote euphorically of their joyful reunion in the field of electoral battle. But the TV cameras so ardently desired by the *Telegram*'s owner showed different feelings: Diefenbaker and Hees sat as far as physically possible from one another on their mutual platform, shared no confidences, exchanged no small talk, and avoided each other's eyes throughout their day of enforced companionship.

Peter Reilly, less easily managed by his boss, quit Bassett's TV empire after only four weeks' employment in 1966, when the publisher threatened to cancel Reilly's programme if Peter refused to share a CTV scoop with the *Telegram*.

Bassett's chief partner and front man in the licence application was Joel Aldred, the best-known commercial announcer on North American television, a totally uncritical worshipper of John Diefenbaker who supported the Chief until the very end, and a bright and versatile businessman with excellent financial connections. The Aldred magic didn't hurt, either. Bassett needed his services in the beginning, and the handsome announcer wasn't fully squeezed out of the TV station he'd sweated to create until it had been on the air for almost six months.

There may have been one Bassett backer with misgivings. A major financial supporter was John David Eaton, heir to the department store fortune, and a man as generous to the Conservative Party of Canada as to Bassett. Legend has it that when the CFTO blueprints were drafted, Eaton insisted the new studio be designed to specifications suitable for palletized storage of his department store's stock, so the building wouldn't be a total waste if the TV enterprise failed.

To round out an acceptable team for his application, Bassett recruited Ted Rogers, son of the Canadian radio pioneer, and perhaps as important, past president of Canada's Young Progressive Conservatives. Bassett's lawyer, Eddie Goodman, had run John Diefenbaker's leadership campaign in Ontario, and was widely regarded as the party's Ontario fixer.

Another go-between in this classic Canadian example of money in search of power via government licencing, was the *Telegram*'s Ottawa correspondent, Peter Dempson, who is quoted by Bassett's (unofficial) biographer, Maggie Siggins, as having "acted as an emissary between Bassett and several cabinet ministers on the matter of the television licence." In his own book of reminiscence, published in 1968, Dempson relates how Diefenbaker, complaining to him about a *Telegram* story in September, 1961, asked how the *Telegram* could be so cruel "after all I've done for your paper." As this confrontation took place three months after granting of CFTO's licence, Dempson wonders whether the PM might have been referring to it, but adds, ingenuously, "But this couldn't be. The BBG was an independent board, its members of different political affiliations."

The Bassett/Aldred/Rogers application, presented to the BBG in Toronto's Union Station on Wednesday morning, March 16, 1960, was not shy on programme promises. There was something for everyone, from a show called "The Toy Shop" to be broadcast to pre-schoolers three times weekly, to a half-hour weekly drama series titled "Toronto Hospital." There was to be a daily comedy and variety show and much, much more. There was to be opera, fine music, and good drama. CFTO promised

Opening day at CFTO. The champagne bubbles temporarily drown out the cash registers as John Bassett (left) toasts his triumph with Ontario Lt. Governor Keiller McKay, Premier Leslie Frost, and the soon-to-be-dumped Joel Aldred. (CTV Television Network)

the BBG that 44.5 per cent of its prime-time telecasts would be made in Canada. But in 1962 only 17.34 per cent of its prime-time shows were Canadian, and 1963 was no better.

The BBG had issued its first regulations in November, 1959, and they included the first formal "Canadian content" rules. In April, 1961 every Canadian TV station was required to have an overall Canadian content of 45 per cent in any week's programming. By April, 1962 the requirement was for 55 per cent Canadian material. The CBC was already over the required minimums; drama was flowering on CBC-TV, as were Norman Campbell's magnificent productions of opera, symphonic music and ballet. But the private stations shouted foul between their public vows of Canadian pie-in-the-sky — later.

The BBG, getting heat from some of the Diefenbaker cabinet, as well as the TV station owners, backed off. Canadian content could be averaged out over four-week periods, instead of being computed every week. In summer, to accommodate lots of cheap, American re-runs, 45 per cent would be ok, even after 1962. Moreover, Canadian content could include foreign broadcasts with "Canadian participation" or those "of general interest to Canadians," such as the World Series or even speeches by the President of the United States. In a later, tougher day, the Canadian Radio-Television Commission engaged in earnest debate over the question of whether Queen Elizabeth could be considered the "Queen of Canada," and whether, therefore, her telecast Christmas greetings could be claimed by CBC as Canadian content. The initial ruling, appealed by CBC, had been that the Queen's broadcast from Sandringham was not a Canadian programme.

Most important to the private broadcasters, the BBG stretched its definition of prime time. Instead of having to include 40 per cent Canadian prime-time programmes between 8 p.m. and 10 p.m., as first proposed, the stations could define prime time as from 6 p.m. until midnight. Thus they could cram the early and late evening hours, poor sources of audience and revenue, with cheap news and quiz shows, meet the regulations, and keep the lucrative, mid-evening slots free for sexy American network shows.

Creation of second stations in major Canadian cities also made development of a private TV network inevitable, after the Canadian Broadcasters' Association's years of fruitless efforts to be permitted a private radio network. When Spence Caldwell, who had managed the CBC's Dominion Radio Network back in 1944, failed in his bid for the Toronto TV licence in March, 1961, he regrouped his forces and asked the BBG that December for permission to establish a TV network instead. The board agreed, provided he could persuade six of the eight new stations to join the network.

Caldwell got the stations, but gave away so much

in the process that the CTV network, when it began in 1961, was financially hamstrung from the start. CTV got only 25 cents of every dollar of network advertising revenue for management, administration and programme production. The remaining 75 cents went back to the affiliated stations. By comparison, CBC keeps 50 per cent of revenue shared with its private affiliates, and the American networks pass only 30 per cent of their commercial dollars back to their affiliates. Caldwell was reduced to producing mostly low-budget quiz shows and talk shows, with a couple of inexpensive variety programmes. By 1965, harrassed both by John Bassett and a group of private station operators who'd formed a competitive group, the Independent Television Organization, through which they pooled resources to buy American programmes, Caldwell was on the ropes. He gave up, and the private affiliates immediately asked the BBG to let *them* run the network as a co-operative.

In the meantime Mike Pearson, now prime minister, and his secretary of state, Maurice Lamontagne, had brought back Robert Fowler to produce yet another report on broadcasting. In his second report, completed in September, 1965, Fowler and his committee (which included Marc Lalonde, who was later Prime Minister Trudeau's closest advisor) came down hard against a network operated by the private TV stations. Well aware of the heavy programming of such stunning American shows as "Leave It To Beaver," "I Love Lucy," "The Rifleman," "Wagon Train," and "Boston Blackie," Fowler said the CTV affiliates "have not shown themselves competent or responsible enough to discharge this responsibility." Commenting on the "unsavoury feud" between CTV and the affiliates, Fowler said the stations "in their jealous concern that outside investors in CTV should not make a profit... have curtailed the means for CTV to provide an adequate national service."

But on February 23, 1966 "Fast Eddie" Goodman appeared before the BBG again and soothed the board's anxieties. The new CTV, he said, would serve Canadians magnificently, not least through a new programme series to be titled "Omnibus," televising the world's finest offerings of culture: drama, opera, symphony orchestras, ballet. The BBG needed just two weeks to agree to formation of the new, co-operative network. The affiliates got their toy, and a place in bed with the elephant of private broadcasting, CFTO, which was to dominate the network through its huge audiences, sophisticated production facilities and bombastic owner. In 1980 Canadians were still waiting for "Omnibus." But as drama critic Nathan Cohen had written of private TV submissions to the BBG in 1963, "(they) were hilarious fantasies to everyone except the members of the Board of Broadcast Governors."

Ernie Bushnell had a shot, too, at development of a mini-network, but it foundered on a complex series of financial deals and BBG approvals.

A third network began with the first telecast, on January 6, 1974, of the Global TV Network. Global was the brainchild and creation of Al Bruner, the original sales manager at Bassett's CFTO. Bruner had been squeezed out of the CFTO operation at the same time as Joel Aldred, and had gone to CHCH Hamilton, the impertinent "David" of the Toronto TV market, taking many of his richest commercial accounts with him. By the end of the sixties, Al Bruner, an irrepressible entrepreneur and visionary, wanted to take on CTV on its home turf, and compete directly with it in Toronto and Ottawa.

At least some of Al Bruner's indisputable gifts as a salesman stemmed from his total inability to

Al Bruner: never a small gesture when a large one would do just as well. (Global TV)

conceive of half-measures. His concept for Global was no exception. To run the news department he hired Bill Cunningham. Cunningham, a former CBC correspondent and producer of CBC-TV's "Newsmagazine," had been a mainstay of the CBC news department in the sixties. He had bossed the CBC "National News" for a period, and come close to overcoming the petty union disputes that prevented it ever becoming an exciting programme, before he was professionally assassinated by his colleagues and shunted into a backwater while being treated in hospital for the bleeding ulcer he had developed in the service of the CBC. Arguably Canada's classiest and brightest TV news journalist and producer, Cunningham by himself was enough to ensure an exciting service for Global viewers.

Patrick Watson was hired to produce the stunning series "Witness To Yesterday," in which actors, costumed and briefed as great historical figures, were interviewed by Watson and required, spon-

Bill Cunningham with Cambodian troops in the sixties. Maybe the classiest of them all. (CBC Archives)

taneously, to account for their actions and careers. And then there was Don Harron, Canada's wittiest and least repressible comic, who was asked to produce a send-up of the news from Ottawa.

Bruner sent to England and repatriated Bernie Braden, by then a household name, literally, in British TV. Braden was given *carte blanche* to develop a late-night, five-day-a-week variety show. Next Bruner turned to Pierre Berton, clearly Canada's best-known and most-respected TV public affairs personality. Berton, the prolific author, formerly the toughest newspaper columnist and magazine editor in the country, and an unremitting

Canadian patriot and history buff, was assigned a show, "My Canada," in which he could use his formidable story-telling gifts to bring national history to life for his viewers. And there were others, many others. Al Bruner, a man possessed, was actually going to do what all the others had promised.

Then there were the studios. Built inside the former warehouse of a heavy equipment company, Global's studios and offices made the word sumptuous seem tame, stale and inadequate. There were hanging plants everywhere, sweeping vistas between cantilevered office mezzanines and spaces below, curving corridors, conference rooms (by the score, it seemed) with custom-built board tables of Brobdignagian proportions, and an executive office suite calculated to bring tears to the eyes of an NBC vice-president.

And the equipment! Al only wanted the best. From the VTR rooms and telecine chains to the control rooms and cameras, the best was all he bought. The huge newsroom was a studio itself, complete with lighting grid and sets from which reporters could literally turn from their typewriters and copy desks to the live studio cameras, carrying the clatter of teletype machines behind the impact of news coming straight from the editing desk to the viewer's livingroom.

Global was, like "Seven Days" before it, brash, slick, glossy, cheeky — and within weeks, virtually bankrupt. The founding force of Global had begun work, during the summer of 1973, in the old Lord Simcoe Hotel on Toronto's King Street. Theirs were the only TV offices (all converted hotel rooms) where every producer had his own john and shower, and where most adjourned to the lobby bar for bloody marys as soon as the clock struck noon each working day. The move into the stunning new

*Babylon in TV-land;
some of Global's office
space. (Global TV;
DOFASCO of Hamilton
photograph)*

*The Global reception
area. Calculated to
bring tears to the eyes.
(DOFASCO of Hamilton)*

building on Barber Greene Road in north-east
Toronto only added to the enchantment, until the
day it was discovered the banks weren't prepared
to cover the payroll cheques. What Bruner wasn't,
it developed, was a great administrator. Less than
12 weeks after Global hit the airwaves Bruner was
gone; a new, hard-nosed group of managers was in
place; and Global TV had begun the rolling series of

News with pizzaz; putting the teletypes in the livingroom. (DOFASCO of Hamilton)

corporate shuffles, mergers, re-organizations that were to require a revolving door on the executive suite through the network's first decade.

Nevertheless, with third TV stations now broadcasting in many Canadian cities, and despite a continuing attrition of budgets for Canadian programming (which the current managers hoped the CRTC would either not notice or not mention), Global had begun to stretch by the end of the decade. It made affiliate arrangements with a chain of private stations reaching to Vancouver. And if those affiliates, like CTV's, were reluctant to spend money for Canadian programmes, they were at least in small ways adding to the sum of Canadian options available to viewers.

Another viewing choice was also developing at the end of the seventies. Educational TV had developed a permanent foothold, after tiny and tentative beginnings in Ontario and Quebec, and later in British Columbia, Alberta and Saskatchewan. Starting from the modest beginnings of pioneer radio in the twenties and thirties, and going on to use CBC school broadcasts, the provinces had begun to explore and develop real TV studios and networks of their own.

Whatever the complaints of Canadian television viewers in the late seventies and early eighties — and they were many, and frequently justified — lack of choice wasn't among them, at least in the heavily populated parts of the country. The most frequent sound in the family rooms of Canadian homes with children was the click of TV channel selectors, as the young folk scoured the airwaves for suitable viewing.

The Triumph of Technology over Creativity: 1970-...

In 1968, as one of her last acts in parliament, Judy LaMarsh piloted her new Broadcast Act through the House of Commons. The new act replaced the BBG with a Canadian Radio-Television Commission and, for the first time, totally divested the government of any licencing authority, giving it all to the CRTC. But without the long-term funding arrangements contained in early drafts of the legislation, most of its provisions did little more than add cosmetic improvement to the situation of Canadian broadcasting. Miss LaMarsh poured champagne for her staff the night the new Broadcast Act was given royal assent. The Broadcast Act was to be her final parliamentary legacy to Canada. But it had less fizz than the celebratory cocktails and was flat as soon.

Al Bruner had *almost* proved that Canadian television programming could be fresh, innovative, exciting. He'd been done in by a combination of factors: his own wild incompetence as an administrator; the emergence of the 1973-74 energy crunch that drastically forced Global's start-up costs through the roof; over-spending on facilities and offices; a series of almost criminally inept purchases of the biggest losers available from Hollywood feature film producers (all lovingly bought by a Global employee who was actually paid a commission on each purchase!).

But most significantly, having made the wilfully

foolish decision to attempt commencement of a new TV season in January, instead of using the traditional, September starting date, Bruner, by the very act of creating Global, alerted the American networks to the potential value of the Canadian market. Until 1974 Canada had been the beneficiary of American network "dumping" of their programme series. The production costs were already covered by the American sponsors, so NBC, CBS and ABC let the programmes go as re-runs at loss-leader prices, happily paid by CBC and CTV. But with a third network in Canada, even though it was at the time confined to Ontario, there was a chance to develop a real auction system. Suddenly the commerce in American TV shows became a sellers' market and prices shot up. That's what Global, among its competitors, is mostly known for. After all of Al Bruner's fond dreams for Canadian production, Global is remembered as the "spoiler," the upstart who caused financial hardship for everybody else.

Canada at the end of the seventies was still the biggest and best market in the world for American programmes. It was also, on a per capita basis, paying the highest prices. In 1977, for example, Japan, with five times Canada's population, paid an average of $3,000 to $3,500 per half hour of purchased American programming. Canada that year paid an average of $4,500 to $6,000 for the same shows. Countries with populations similar to Canada's (Yugoslavia and Colombia, for instance) paid from $175 to $500 for shows like "MASH" and "All In The Family," which sold in Canada for $2,000. In the Toronto area alone, TV stations were paying the American networks close to $20 million every year for TV programmes by the end of the seventies.

While private television was exploding through

the sixties, there was a parallel mushrooming of communications technology. Cable television, the delivery of TV signals to homes over wire, had begun in England in 1948. The first Canadian system, operated by the British Rediffusion Company, started in Montreal in 1952. A London, Ontario, dry cleaner, Ed Jarmain, whose hobby was electronics, decided to improve his TV signal with a receiving tower in his backyard that same year. It worked so well he began selling the service to neighbours, and soon had a burgeoning CATV business (as cable came to be called) in London and several other small Ontario cities.

Cable wasn't "broadcasting," of course; the signals were actually sent over cables, so the government originally saw no need or right to regulate and licence the new industry. But by 1968, with TV stations screaming foul, the newly appointed CRTC moved into the field with the first regulations of cable distribution. Cable, after all, could give Canadian viewers those money-making American programmes directly from the American networks. So why watch CBC or CTV to see them?

Cable obviously had many economic advantages to its now-licenced operators. The programmes, simply plucked from the air, cost nothing after installation of the primary receivers. Income, based on weekly or monthly fees to users, was constant, growing and sure. Nobody in cable had to be concerned with ratings; people either subscribed to the service or they didn't. And more Canadians, proportionately, subscribed to cable than citizens of any other nation. By 1977 only 15 per cent of American homes with television also had cable. In Canada, which had started later, already half the homes with TV sets were wired into cable systems. As the technology improved, more channels were added, until by 1979, 20 channels could be selected on home converters in Toronto, along with several more carrying the cable company public service offerings.

By then, too, the CRTC was insisting that all new and renewed cable connections be built with two-way wire to accommodate future development of data retrieval; push button, home referenda operated by government; shopping from home via computer; and the multitude of other wonders promised by accelerating research into satellite communications, computer technology and optical fibre waveguides. These latter threads, typically just six thousandths of an inch thick, could carry up to a half million one-way voice circuits as compared with 36,000 circuits on a coaxial cable thicker than a man's thumb.

Spinning glass into gold. The new optical fibre waveguides; 500,000 messages through the eye of a needle. The coaxial cable beside it became the ox-cart of electronics. (Department of Communications)

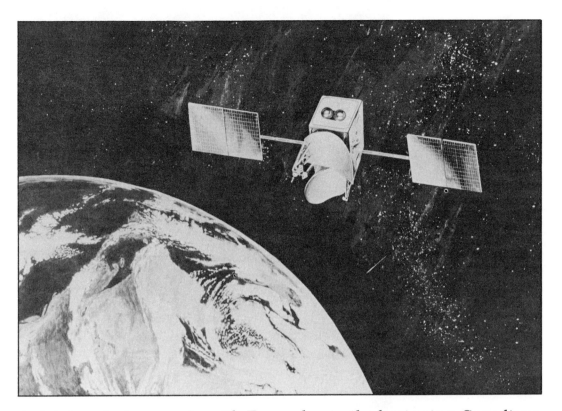

Anik B, launched in December, 1978. (Department of Communications)

As with Fessenden in the beginning, Canadians were well ahead in many areas of the new technologies. Starting with Alouette and the first Anik satellites of the sixties and early seventies, Canada had devised and built equipment a technical generation ahead of anything else in the world. Under the guidance of John Chapman, who'd written the definitive report on satellite communications in 1968, Canada's eighth satellite, the Hermes, launched in 1976 by NASA, was the most powerful stationary communications spacecraft yet built. And although Canada was dependent on the United States for the powerful rocket delivery vehicles, it was our electronics packages that were pioneering most areas of satellite communications. The Canadian Telesat Corporation became a world leader in commercial satellite utilization.

Launching Anik: Canadian technology riding a U.S. rocket to a tête-à-tête 22,000 miles above Hudson's Bay. (Department of Communciations)

NASA *specialists inspecting Canada's satellite communications package prior to a launch aboard a Delta rocket. The Canadian satellite equipment, with transmission power from ten to twenty times greater than that of anything else in use, was years ahead of the state-of-the-art in the U.S. and elsewhere. (Department of Communications)*

By the time of his death in September, 1979, John Chapman was on a new crusade: direct home reception of space satellite TV. Early equipment involved only a four-foot receiver "dish" and a small black box containing the electronics package needed to convert the satellite signals into pictures on a home set. First models, built in Canada, cost $3,500 apiece, but with longer production runs a unit cost of $500 seemed within reach.

But as with colour television sets, and later home videotape equipment, market penetration was diminishing with each new development. In the beginning, television broadcasts cost viewers only about five cents an hour, including the

John Chapman with a model of the Hermes satellite. (Department of Communications)

A dish antenna and electronics package which can bring direct, colour TV reception to individual homes from satellites. The converter unit atop the TV set translates the satellite signals into home viewing. (Department of Communications)

subsidies of CBC and programme costs. Cable doubled that figure; colour television jacked up the costs some more. Home VTR equipment, pay TV, video disc players, home satellite receivers, data retrieval and the like could only raise the costs on an exponential curve.

Because of cost, cable and colour television were accepted in Canadian homes much more slowly than were the initial black-and-white television sets. In 1980 it was estimated that there would be at least a ten-year lag while the newest toy, videotape or whatever, moved from use in 10 per cent of TV homes to 50 per cent. Given similar subscriber resistance to the other sophisticated new consumer aids, the turn of the century seemed an optimistic target date for home data retrieval or computer shopping among the general population.

While all of that was going on out there in television land, radio had rediscovered itself and grown in wit, maturity and service. Canadian content rules, finally applied to radio broadcasting, had created almost overnight a staggeringly successful music industry in the country.

When Prime Minister Joe Clark attended the Commonwealth Conference in Lusaka in 1979, CBC technicians Dean Hayward and Carlos Schonfeldt (in light sweater) put together an ad hoc transmitter from which they fed videotape cassettes directly to a satellite for virtually instant transmission to Canada. (Private collection: author)

At the end of the seventies there were more cable television companies in Canada than daily newspapers. But radio was expanding again, too. It had found new life and new voices, with CBC programmes like Peter Gzowski's "This Country In The Morning," and Barbara Frum's "As It Happens."

Peter Gzowski at work on "This Country in the Morning." (CBC Archives)

Largely ignored by both the politicians and the corporate bureaucrats who seemed intent on keeping TV programming safe, not to say emasculated, the best of CBC radio was a world leader in public affairs broadcasting by 1980. "As It Happens" was the brightest, most feisty and topical daily inter-

Barbara Frum and Alan Maitland; every evening a celebration "As It Happens". (CBC Archives)

view show on English-language radio heard anywhere. Cheeky and irreverent, it had come to rank with the staid and prestigious *Globe and Mail* newspaper as a force to be considered by the Ottawa power brokers of the seventies; few of them had the courage or temerity to refuse an invitation to chat with hostess Barbara Frum.

The "Sunday Morning" programme, three hours of weekly review and analysis of national and global events, provided a standard against which all other such broadcasts had to be measured. While TV was still largely distracted with simply polishing old techniques, "Sunday Morning" was

"Sunday Morning" producer Marc Starowicz (standing) with programme hosts Patrick Martin and Bronwyn Drainie. (CBC Archives)

breaking new ground in radio documentary production, building multi-textured sound presentations a quantum leap beyond those it had succeeded. While CBC radio news editors were content to rebroadcast the same pedestrian newscasts with the same stories read in the same order, for three, four or more successive hourly broadcasts, day in and day out, "As It Happens" and "Sunday Morning" and their like were making broadcasting *an event*. Their staffs still believed in sewing the extra stitch, walking the extra mile, taking the additional pains. They were proving broadcasting could still strike sparks and sound resonances in its listeners.

TV stations were busy developing identi-kit news readers, indistinguishable in their tailored blazers, plummy reading style and air-blown hair styles. They were equally at home in Toronto, Saskatoon or Salt Lake City. But radio, having finally thrown off the stereotypes of the forties and fifties, was finding some time for reflection and some affection for a few rough edges, even the giddy uncertainty, again, of some live programming. Taking all the wrong cues from "big brother" TV, however, radio producers were trying to package and polish their shows via slick, contrived and edited tape parcelling.

In television, cable, regarded as The Enemy for its fragmentation of audiences, effectually gave the visual medium the same opportunity already grasped by radio, that of programming for selected portions of the potential audience. "Majority" audiences were beyond reach now anyhow, given the multiplicity of choice. So why not make TV programmes for carefully targeted special-interest groups and serve those constituencies better? The lowest common denominator was dead anyhow; long live the rule of quality programming designed for particular sections of the public. TV producers agonized over the attrition of audience loyalty, but it was there for any programming with some relevance to the individuals who, as those same producers seemed to forget in their pursuit of "big numbers," made up every audience. Executives and viewers lamented the dearth of creative people; many of them, Canadians, were busy producing American programmes like "MASH," "Laugh-In," "The Smothers Brothers," "Carol Burnett," and the like.

The unhappy truth, by 1980, was that the technical and electronic improvements proceeded with a direct, inverse diminution of the real spark in Canadian TV. The administrators had won. It

© 1967. Reprinted with permission of the *Toronto Star* Syndicate

"Th-Thats All Folks."

Mike Pearson denied TV coverage of parliament to Canadians. Pierre Trudeau relented and some wondered if MP's were being programmed to prefer performance to principle in the daily, televised question periods. Nothing would ever be the same. (Duncan MacPherson in the Toronto Star)

Anne Murray (centre), the first international star 'made' by CBC television. For once the Canadian aversion to the vulgarity of success was overcome by delight in an engaging personality. (CBC Archives)

had stopped being an adventure for most, and become a business. The sound persisted, more mellow and modulated than ever, but the fury was gone. The Ernie Bushnells, the Norman DePoes, Peter Reillys, Laurier LaPierres, Ross MacLeans and their like were mostly gone — dead, retired, or just openly weary. The fires in the belly had been put out by the water torture of bureaucratic memo-writers. We could just about remember the words of those first, exciting anthems of creation; but it was as if we'd lost our ear for the music.

Epilogue

Broadcasting, by 1980, had done as much to transform society and government as, centuries earlier, the printing press and the development in industrial society of universal education. The ubiquitous microphones and cameras of the post-fifties had forced a whole new order of responsiveness on governments, had literally re-created a sense-of-the-meeting potential in democratic societies. Now gross examples of gunboat diplomacy and international power politics were possible only for monolithic (or desperate) authoritarian states, as the Soviets in Hungary, Czechoslovakia, Afghanistan. But the British and French had to get out of Egypt in 1956; it was just too embarrassing being caught in the act of military blackmail by TV journalists whose reports were generating instant daily reaction among the voters back in Brittany and Sussex.

Television's very existence dictated that Bull Connors could not survive as sheriff of Selma, Alabama; it was public response to the televised fire hoses and alsatians he turned on peaceful black marchers that spelled his end and their triumph. So with the U.S. military adventures in Viet Nam, the last terms in office of Presidents Lyndon Johnson and Richard Nixon. All the image builders in the world were inadequate to negate TV's capacity to cut through hypocrisy and expose reality.

More than 2,300 years after Plato, radio and television had re-invented the town meeting; well used, each could help voters make the gut decisions essential in the selection of government leaders. In a world grown too big, too complex, TV sometimes let us see beyond the public masks of public men. Television was our best, often our only chance to penetrate the self-serving rhetoric, to glimpse the shiny upper lip, downcast glance, perturbation of the pretenders seeking our electoral favour. Some consummate political actors, it's true, could occasionally outwit even the merciless glass eye given us to examine them. But that had been as true in Plato's day; as least we could again see them, close up.

Television transformed print reporting, too. No one watching a videotape replay of Lee Harvey Oswald taking three bullets in the groin at the hand of Jack Ruby had any need of an eyewitness account of the shooting. Newspapers abandoned most eyewitness stories; they turned to analysis and commentary and thereby made our flow of information immensely more rich.

Ironically, years after our newspapers had been forced by the impact of TV actuality reporting to move heavily into interpretive journalism, broadcast reporters still scarcely noted the subsequent public appetite for more analytical and subjective material. Like all converts to a new faith, TV programmers are conservative to a fault, myopically married to traditions younger than themselves, too busy aping yesterday's successes to note today's needs. Dogma and cant are everything; "repeat after me" is the prayer of invocation. "Sixty Minutes" was successful; "Mary Tyler Moore" was successful; "The Johnny Carson Show" was successful. So better smudged copies of those than experimental ventures over the edges of the flat earth horizons of TV executive offices.

None of the foregoing, unhappily, takes note of the notion that television audiences have progressed beyond the communications kiddie-cars provided by early TV. In the beginning, novelty alone was enough. Even now actuality is unmatched and exciting. Whether in the slow-motion replays of a football game, the underwater grace of the olympic swimmer, or the stunned expression of the election-night politician conceding defeat, the cameras still make real events proximate and compelling. But that isn't enough.

In the easy, uncritical early days, when television earned impact just by its existence, producers learned that shock could be used to stir the first jaded audiences. Sound and picture edits were planned to jolt viewers back to a state of total attention; military atrocities and culturally sanctioned bare breasts were equally revered as "grabbers" in a dull documentary. Guilt was shovelled at audiences in miles of film detailing the squalor and obscenity of life in slums, on Indian reserves, in medieval public institutions. But the public had a curious subconscious response to such film: in effect, the documentaries gave their viewers a social catharsis, a purge of conscience. "I felt so bad while I was watching that show," said the subconscious mind. "And I feel so much better now that I've had that experience." So the viewers wore their electronic hair shirts for thirty minutes, or sixty, and shucked them, along with any sense of personal responsibility, during the closing credits and commercials.

Our world is hip-deep in information overload; we've all learned to block out or ignore everything which seems less than vital or relevant. Some radio programming was finding a way past those mental checks and blocks by the end of the seventies, but almost no television. Spectacle isn't enough to provoke response anymore. Now it takes genuine vitality and imagination, true wit and clear relevance to the interests and needs of individual viewers who, after all, watch television in groups of one — individuals before and after everything else.

Before TV can again strike echoes in its audience, it will need to take soundings from that audience; consumer advocacy, in the broadest sense, matters now. So does clear and committed dissection of the obfuscation and hypocrisy of much of public, corporate and institutional rhetoric. Too many Canadian students know that much of their life in school is, in the word of systems analysts, disfunctional; too many factory workers know colleagues are contracting occupational diseases like asbestiosis; too many shoppers know that advertising claims are often arrant nonsense; too many voters know that politicians tell a lot of lies; too many TV viewers know that programme producers are more interested in ratings than content.

Burgeoning technology offers hope: the home satellite receivers, the two-way wire and the fibre optics make new initiatives possible. New frontiers have always attracted the adventurous, the innovative, the reckless. Maybe, in the eighties and nineties, broadcasting will find its new Lindberghs. They're overdue.

Bibliography

The Aird Report. *1929. Report of the Royal Commission on Broadcasting.* Ottawa: Government of Canada.

ALLARD, T. J. 1979. *Straight Up.* Ottawa: The Canadian Communications Foundation.

ARCHER, GLEASON L. 1938. *History of Radio to 1926.* Washington, D.C.: The American Historical Society, Inc.

Broadcast Committee of the House of Commons. *Report on the White Paper of 1966.* Ottawa: Government of Canada.

The Canadian Association for Adult Education. 1954. *Education in Public Affairs Radio.*

Canadian Institute on Public Affairs. 1968. *The Image of the Issue.*

The Canadian Radio and Television Annual. 1950. Oshawa: Mundy-Goodfellow.

CBC. 1933-1979. *Annual Reports.*

————. *1939, 1942, 1943. Broadcast Schedules* with photographs.

————. 1941-1943. *Five Years of Achievement.*

————. 1946. *A Digest of Statements to the House of Commons Special Committee on Radio Broadcasting in 1946.*

————. 1960. *Broadcasting in Canada.*

————. 1968. *CBC: A Brief History and Background.*

————. 1961. *Chronology of Network Broadcasting in Canada, 1901-1961.*

The CBC and Canadian Broadcasting. 1943. Statements to the Parliamentary Special Committee on Radio Broadcasting. Ottawa: Government of Canada.

Clyne Committee. 1979. *Telecommunications in Canada.* Ottawa: Government of Canada.

CORBETT, EDWARD A. 1957. *We Have With Us Tonight.* Toronto: Ryerson Press.

CREAMER, JOSEPH and ZIFF, DAVIS. 1945. *Radio Sound Effects.* New York: William B. Hoffman.

CRTC Symposium on Violence. 1976. Ottawa.

Davey Report. 1970. *Report of the Special Senate Committee on Mass Media.* Ottawa: Government of Canada.

DEMPSON, PETER. 1968. *Assignment Ottawa.* Toronto: General Publishing.

DESBARATS, PETER. 1976. *Rene.* Toronto: McClelland and Stewart.

DIEFENBAKER, JOHN G. 1975-1977. *One Canada: Memoirs of the Rt. Hon. John G. Diefenbaker.* Vols. I-III. Toronto: Macmillan.

ELLIS, DAVID. 1979. *Evolution of the Canadian Broadcasting System.* Ottawa: Government of Canada.

Encyclopedia Canadiana. 1968. Montreal: Grolier.

FERGUSON, MAX. 1967. *And Now, Here's Max.* Toronto: McGraw-Hill.

Fowler Commission. 1965. *Report of the Committee on Broadcasting.* Ottawa: Government of Canada.

GARRY, RALPH. 1962. *For the Young Viewer.* Toronto: McGraw-Hill.

GORHAM, MAURICE. 1952. *Broadcasting and Television Since 1900.* London: Andrew Dakers Limited.

HALLMAN, E. S. 1977. *Broadcasting in Canada.* Toronto: General Publishing.

IRVING, JOHN, ed. 1962. *The Mass Media in Canada.* Toronto: Ryerson Press.

JACK, DONALD. 1977. *The Story of CFRB.* Toronto: Macmillan.

JAMIESON, DON. 1966. *The Troubled Air.* Fredericton: Brunswick Press.

KOCH, HOWARD. 1970. *The Panic Broadcast.* Boston: Little, Brown.

LAMARSH, JUDY. 1969. *Memoirs of a Bird in a Gilded Cage.* Toronto: McClelland and Stewart.

LAMBERT, RICHARD S. 1940. *Home Front.* Toronto: Ryerson Press.

Manitoba Telephone System. 1937-1948. *Manitoba Calling* Periodicals. Winnipeg.

Massey Commission. 1951. *Report of the Royal Commission on the National Development in the Arts, Letters and Sciences.* Ottawa: Government of Canada.

McNAUGHT, CARLTON. 1940. *Canada Gets the News.* Toronto: Ryerson Press.

Parliamentary Broadcasting Committee Reports. 1932-1961. Ottawa: Government of Canada.

PAWLEY, A. E. 1975. *Broadcast from the Front.* Toronto: Samuel-Stevens.

PEARSON, LESTER B. 1972-1975. *Mike: Memoirs of the Rt. Hon. Lester B. Pearson. Vols.* I-III. Toronto: University of Toronto Press.

PEERS, FRANK W. 1969. *The Politics of Canadian Broadcasting.* Toronto: University of Toronto Press.

PELLETIER, HON. GERARD, Minister of Communications. 1973. *Proposals for a Communications Policy for Canada.* Ottawa: Government of Canada.

Report of the Royal Commission on Broadcasting. Vol. I. 1957. Ottawa: Government of Canada.

ROLO, CHARLES J. 1963. *Radio Goes to War.* London: Faber and Faber.

ROSEN, EARL, and WHELPDALE, ELIZABETH, eds. 1969. *Educational Television Across Canada.* Toronto: Metropolitan Educational Television Association.

RUTHERFORD, PAUL. 1978. *The Making of the Canadian Media.* Toronto: McGraw-Hill Ryerson.

SAMNER, D. B. 1949. The Canadian Broadcasting Corporation. MA Dissertation at Queen's University, Kingston, Ontario.

SCHRAMM, WILBUR; LYLE, JACK; and PARKER, EDWIN B. 1961. *Television in the Lives of our Children.* Toronto: University of Toronto Press.

SIGGINS, MAGGIE. 1979. *Bassett.* Toronto: James Lorimer.

SINGER, BENJAMIN and GREEN, LYNDSAY. 1977. *The Social Functions of Radio in a Community Emergency.* Toronto: Copp Clark.

STEWART, SANDY. 1975. *A Pictorial History of Radio in Canada.* Toronto: Gage.

STURSBERG, PETER. 1971. *Mister Broadcasting.* Toronto: Peter Martin.

TURNBULL, R. B. 1951. *Radio and TV Sound Effects.* London: Reinhardt and Co.

TWOMEY, JOHN. 1978. *Canadian Broadcasting History Resources.* CBC.

UNESCO. 1954. *Canada's Farm Radio Forum.*

White Paper on Broadcasting. 1966. Ottawa: Government of Canada.

Index